THE KING OF THE KOSHER GROCERS

by Joe Minjares

S A M U E L   F R E N C H ,   I N C .

45 WEST 25TH STREET   NEW YORK 10010

7623 SUNSET BOULEVARD   HOLLYWOOD 90046

LONDON   *TORONTO*

**Dedicated to
the great American cities
and
the people who never left the
neighborhood**

IMPORTANT BILLING AND CREDIT REQUIREMENTS

All producers of THE KING OF THE KOSHER GROCERS *must* give credit to the Author of the Play in all programs distributed in connection with performances of the Play and in all instances in which the title of the Play appears for purposes of advertising, publicizing or otherwise exploiting the Play and/or a production. The name of the Author *must* also appear on a separate line, on which no other name appears, immediately following the title, and *must* appear in size of type not less than fifty percent the size of the title type.

THE KING OF THE KOSHER GROCERS was first presented by the Mixed Blood Theatre Company. The play opened on September 30, 1992 with the following cast:

Jacinto "Joe" Chavez...................Joe Minjares
Elvis Mooney ....Warren C. Bowles
Isadore "Izzie" Silvers ....Michael Tezla
Jamar Mooney .... Kevin Linell
Lenora Kaufman.................Marquetta Senters
Billy Moss...................... Michael Greenfield
Earl Lewis........................... Jay Hornbacher

Produced by Jack Reuler, Artistic Director
Directed by Marion McClinton
Scenery Designed by Nayna Ramey
Scenery Constructed by Dan Fritsche
Scenery Dressed by Dwight Callaway
Sound Designed by Herbie Woodruff
Lighting Designed and Operated by Scott Peters
Costumes Designed by Chris Cook
Stage Managed by Dwight Callaway
Creative Consultant: Tomas Benitez

CHARACTERS

Jacinto "Joe" Chavez – 70s. Born in Mexico, raised in Texas. Speaks with a slight accent. His bad knees bear witness to his years of working in the sugar beet fields. He is feisty, lovable and very sensitive.

Elvis Mooney – 70s. Born in Macon Georgia, the tall, lanky African American is tired, reserved and lonely. His quick temper often betrays his usually demure personality.

Isadore "Izzie" Silvers – 70s. Owner of Market. He is a hard-working, spry and quick-witted second generation Russian Jew. His caustic sense of humor is often misunderstood. He tends to be impatient but has a heart of gold.

Jamar Mooney – 19. Grandson of Elvis Mooney. He is charming yet intense. His dreams put fire in his eyes. Sometimes moody like his grandfather. Even in jeans he is elegant.

Lenora Kaufman – 30s. The overly officious City Electrical Inspector. Short, slightly overweight, cynical and devious. No one likes her, except the playwright. (Originally written as a male— Leroy.)

(cont.)

Billy Moss – 20s. Jamar's best friend. He is dynamic, restless and goes through life full blast.

Earl Lewis – 50s. The head of inspections. He is a heavy set, slightly balding, ominous-looking man. Under his rough exterior is a good ole boy who never takes things too seriously.

TIME & PLACE

North Minneapolis

The present

THE KING OF THE KOSHER GROCERS

The play takes place in North Minneapolis. The time is present. We see the interior of Silvers' Grocery Store. It is a rundown grocery that Izadore Silvers has owned for fifty years. It is morning and SILVERS is opening for the day's business as JAMAR is seen working in the background.

Theme MUSIC as LIGHTS come up, SILVERS is finishing counting his till and goes to the door to turn over the sign to show he is open. HE moves to the side counter to check the coffee percolator as MOONEY enters. The BELL over the door signals his arrival. MOONEY is a 75-year-old black man who, although he doesn't look his age, gives it away by his tired ways. MOONEY is dressed the same way he has dressed every day since anyone can remember: dark overcoat, brown suit with a plaid shirt, black belt, black shoes with rubbers and a short-brimmed brown hat with the brim turned up in the front. SILVERS is dressed in black pants and shoes, white shirt with sleeves rolled up and a soiled white apron. In his breast pocket a plastic pen case is loaded with pencils, markers and pens. HE looks his 76 years and then some, but is a sparkplug. BOTH MEN wear bifocals. JAMAR is dressed in jeans, a white polo shirt, a dirty white apron and a baseball cap worn backwards.

MOONEY. Mornin' Mr. Silvers.

SILVERS. (*Slight Yiddish accent.*) Good morning, Mr. Mooney.

MOONEY. (*Goes for a bag of rock salt by the door.*) I swear, Izzee, you're gonna forget to salt down your sidewalk one too many times and someone's gonna fall and break a hip.

SILVERS. (*Shouting to Mooney, who is now outside.*) I was just going to do it!

(*PHONE rings. It is Milley, Silvers' wife. Her constant phone calls are part of Silvers' daily routine and he knows her ring.*)

SILVERS. Hello sweetheart, yes, sweetheart I'm at the store, I made it fine ... yes, it is chilly ... I love you, too. Bye. (*Hangs up goes to small chalk board next to cash register and makes mark. HE is keeping count of Milley's calls. It is the old men's daily lottery, guess the number of calls by Milley.*)

MOONEY. (*Coming back in.*) Just what you need. Someone breaking a hip and suing you and collecting all that insurance money just 'cuz you forgot to salt down your sidewalk.

SILVERS. Good. At least someone would make some money off of this place. I hope the person that falls down and breaks their hip needs the money. I hope they break two hips and collects double. God bless them.

MOONEY. Got the coffee brewin'?

SILVERS. Jamar put it on.

MOONEY. (*Pours coffee in his mug that he has brought along with his newspaper. Sits and opens paper.*) Got's ta have my coffee first thing. Damn! It's kind of chilly out there.

SILVERS. March in Minnesota and it's chilly?

MOONEY. Uff da, must have had a lapse of memory. (*BOTH chuckle.*) Damn weatherman on TV don't know what the hell they're talking about. Said last night it was supposed to be eighty-five and sunny today.

SILVERS. What! Eighty-five and sunny? It's March for God's sakes. I don't think you heard him right.

MOONEY. I know what I heard, goddamn it. I ain't that damn old that I can't hear. Sat down there and heard it myself. Came on after the fight. Jamar was there. He heard it, too. Tell him Jamar.

JAMAR. That's what he said, Gramps, but we were watching a video tape I recorded last summer.

SILVERS. Oh! Eighty-five and sunny. I see.

MOONEY. (*Trying to save face.*) But that's what he said. Right Jamar? Eighty-five and sunny, right?

JAMAR That's what he said.

MOONEY. There, see. (*Back to paper.*)

(*PHONE rings.*)

SILVERS. Silvers' Market! ... Oh good morning, Jerry.

MOONEY. (*To self*) I didn't say I believed it, I just said I heard it.

SILVERS. ... Yes fine thanks, and how is the family? ... Good glad to hear that ... No, Jerry. We won't be needing anything this week ... No, business is good ... Yes ... Yes ... Well ah ... Oh! I see. (*Lowers voice.*) ... Well could you redeposit the check ... Oh ... Uh huh ... Uh huh ... Well, this is very embarrassing Jerry. This has never happened before ... Well then why don't you have the driver send over a case of ... (*Looks around.*) disposable diapers and ... generic ... yes generic, a case of toilet paper ... generic, and let's see? Oh! A case of Kotex ... yes, the hefty size and that would also be generic ... Good and I'll give the driver a new check and we'll be all set ... Okay, Jerry ... Okay, thanks ... Bye ... Okay, well these things happen, stop apologizing. Forget about it ... Bye. (*Hangs up.*) Disposable diapers, toilet paper and Kotex, great. A delicatessen whose biggest sellers cater to bodily functions. Oy vey!

MOONEY. Problem?

SILVERS. You could say that yes ...

(*PHONE rings.*)

SILVERS. Yes sweetheart? ... Oh, let's see. You fell in love with the milk man? ... Ahhh, you made a mistake in the checkbook, and you're afraid Jerry's check might bounce? ... Oh, just a wild guess ... It'll be okay sweetheart, bye. (*Hangs up and goes to the chalkboard and marks call.*)

MOONEY. (*About chalkboard.*) How'd we end up yesterday?

SILVERS. Let's see ... she made fourteen calls. I guessed fourteen. You owe me a dollar.

MOONEY. Damn! You always win. Well, here's your dollar and one in the kitty for today. Put me down for twelve calls today. No wait, if you're bouncing checks all over town better put me down for fifteen.

SILVERS. (*Goes to put both his and Mooney's number on the board.*) We're not bouncing checks all over town. One check only ... so far. I'm just glad it was with Jerry and not one of the others.

MOONEY. You been doing business with Jerry a long time. As long as I can remember.

SILVERS. Jerry's a good man.

MOONEY. Yes. He is.

SILVERS. His business is growing but he's still a hands-on operator. On the phone every day.

MOONEY. That's why his business is growing.

SILVERS. (*To Jamar.*) Let this be a lesson to you, son. Pick your purveyors carefully. Don't let anyone fool you, service is more important than price and if you are loyal to them, they will be loyal to you and stick by you when times are tough.

MOONEY. I know that's right. When times are good every schmuck on the street is your friend.

SILVERS. Wait a second. Did you just say schmuck? I say schmuck, you don't.

MOONEY. Last week I heard you say "dude." If you can say dude, I can say schmuck.

JAMAR. I'm going to finish the shoveling now, Mr. Silvers.

MOONEY. You better before someone falls and breaks a hip.

SILVERS. I know, Mooney. Why don't you fall and break your hip and sue me. Then you can collect the insurance money and buy me out. Then, I'll go on vacation for two years and come back. Then I'll fall and break my hip, sue you, and buy my business back.

(MOONEY places his hand on Silvers' head to feel for a fever.)

SILVERS. Joking! Joking! It's my first joke of the day.

MOONEY. You shouldn't be joking about things like that Izzie, I mean the way ...

SILVERS. Drink your coffee.

MOONEY. Mrs. Goldstein called in her order yet?

SILVERS. Not yet.

(PHONE rings.)

SILVERS. *(Delighted.)* There she is.

MOONEY. Just like clockwork.

SILVERS. *(Answers.)* Good morning. Silvers' Market. *(Pause.)* Good morning Mrs. Goldstein. How are you today? ... Well, I'm fine thank you ... Milley couldn't be better thank you ... Is your daughter enjoying her visit? ... Oh? That's too bad ... I know, well, you should have told her to come when she could have stayed longer ... I know ... I know ... Well at least she knows you're still alive. I should be so lucky. My sons? They forget the phone rings both ways ... I know ... I know ... I know ... *(Holds hand over phone, to Mooney.)* Mrs. Goldstein is depressed.

MOONEY. Her daughter had to go home early huh?

SILVERS. I know.

MOONEY. That's too bad. Tell her I said hi.

SILVERS. I know ... Elvis says hello, Mrs. Goldstein. (*Listens.*) Mrs. Goldstein says hello. She wants to know how your bladder infection is?

MOONEY. (*A little embarrassed.*) Tell her the burning stopped, the chicken soup she gave me worked fine, just fine.

(*Enter JOE CHAVEZ wearing 1930's style flop hat, plaid shirt and t-shirt, under his winter coat, dark work trousers, work shoes, white socks and bifocals. HE is carrying brown bag containing flour tortillas.*)

SILVERS. The chicken soup did the trick, Mrs. Goldstein.

CHAVEZ. Chingao! It's cold out there!! The TV weatherman was right for a change.

SILVERS. (*Covers the phone.*) Mooney says it's supposed to be eighty-five and sunny.

MOONEY. I did not say ... forget it ... mornin' compadre.

CHAVEZ. Buenos dias, Elvis, Hey Izzie! I owe you a dollar.

SILVERS. (*Nods to Chavez.*) I know ... I know.

CHAVEZ. Tortillas!!! They're still hot, hot off the comale. (*Opens bag and gives one to Mooney.*)

MOONEY. Yes, they are.

(*CHAVEZ goes to counter and starts arranging fresh flour tortillas in plastic bags next to cash register.*)

CHAVEZ. (*To Mooney about tortillas.*) Well, Mr. Quality Control?

MOONEY. These are the best yet! You and Guadalupe make the best tortillas I ever did taste.

CHAVEZ. (*As HE goes for coffee.*) Thank you, Mr. Mooney.

MOONEY. You're welcome, Mr. Chavez.

(*BOTH laugh.*)

SILVERS. I know.

CHAVEZ. (*About phone conversation.*) Mrs. Goldstein?

MOONEY. Yup. she's depressed this morning. Her daughter flew back to Chicago last night.

CHAVEZ. I thought she was going to stay until next week.

MOONEY. She was.

CHAVEZ. Probably couldn't get in a word edge wise.

SILVERS. I know. (*Makes talking motion with his hand.*)

CHAVEZ. Well, if she's depressed that's good news for Izzie, means she'll be eating a lot for the next few days.

MOONEY. That's what I'm afraid of.

CHAVEZ. As much food as that woman packs in her mouth I'm surprised her tongue has room to talk.

MOONEY. Hey Izzie! You wanna little break?

SILVERS. (*To Mooney.*) That would be nice ... I know ... I know.

MOONEY. (*Takes the phone not missing a beat.*) Uh huh ... uh huh ... I know.

SILVERS. Oy vey! That woman! ... I love her but Joe, I'm convinced that in a former life Mrs. Goldstein drove the Jews out of Egypt.

CHAVEZ. Pobrecita! She's a lonely old woman.

MOONEY. I know.

SILVERS. (*Going about his business.*) Yes, she is. The neighborhood is full of them. Lonely old people sitting by the phone waiting for their children to call. It's a shame Joe, it's a damn shame that people devote their entire life to raising their children, then when they need something in return ...

CHAVEZ. I know.

SILVERS. Nothing special mind you, just a little thank you once and a while.

MOONEY. I know.

SILVERS. A kind word. This is all I'm saying.

CHAVEZ/MOONEY. I know.

MOONEY. Well, you know what they say, Mrs. Goldstein.

ALL. "They don't appreciate you till you're dead and gone."

SILVERS. Amen to that. Thank God for the store or they wouldn't have anyone.

CHAVEZ. I know.

SILVERS. (*Irritated.*) Stop with the I knows already!! I'm not Mrs. Goldstein.

MOONEY. Well, Mrs. Goldstein, what did you need today? ... Of course, I'll be happy to run them right over. You just let old Mooney take your order. (*MOONEY begins writing.*) Uh huh, uh huh.

CHAVEZ. One thing I'll never do Izzie, is put all my huevos in one basket.

SILVERS. (*Confused.*) Do what?

CHAVEZ. Put all my huevos in one basket. You know, depend on my daughter, Rosa, for my happiness.

After Carlos died in Vietnam, we wanted to hang on to Rosa too tight and it caused too many problems.

SILVERS. That's understandable.

CHAVEZ. No, sir. I've only got a few more years left and I'm going to live them for myself ... and for Lupe, of course.

SILVERS. Of course. But it's different for Mexican people, let's face it! Your families stay close to home. Not the Jews. The kids go to school get their degrees and they're gone ... I mean look at the neighborhood. It just proves what I am saying ... all the kids grew up and moved to St. Louis Park and left all us old folks here. I remember when this whole neighborhood was Jewish, everyone spoke Yiddish, English was a second language on Plymouth Avenue. Now, all the temples have become Baptist churches and the schools are full on Passover. In the old days during Passover the classrooms were almost empty and they gave the Christian kids double recess to keep them from getting pissed off. This is all I'm saying.

CHAVEZ. Your families are just victims of economics.

SILVERS. What do you mean economics?

CHAVEZ. Your kids had the money to go to school and move to the suburbs. Your people are celebrating the American Dream, this loneliness is just the hangover. My people haven't been invited to the party yet.

SILVERS. Oh yea! Look around you. This isn't exactly "Lifestyles of the Rich and Famous."

CHAVEZ. I know, that's why we love you, cabron. The world is changing and leaving us behind but you stayed to help us remember what the old Northside used to be like. You're one of us, amigo.

(Pause.)

SILVERS. Did we just share a tender moment?

CHAVEZ. Yes. *(Pause.)* Now! Can I have my tortilla money?

SILVERS. No! ... I'll give you Guadalupe's tortilla money, she does all the work. You're just the bagman.

CHAVEZ. But a very good bagman.

SILVERS. That you are, Mr. Chavez, that you are. *(SILVERS goes to till to get Chavez's tortilla money.)*

MOONEY. Great! Mrs. Goldstein, I'll have your groceries over to you within the hour ... Okay bye .. Yea, bye ... within the hour ... I know ... I know ... Okay, bye. *(Hangs up.)* Damn! Is my ear bleeding? Lord, can that woman talk.

SILVERS. Look at me, will you? I used to be the king of the kosher grocers and here I am selling tortillas.

MOONEY. Don't forget the collard greens and black eyed peas, Izzie.

SILVERS. Yes and the sweet potato pie and the jalapeno peppers.

CHAVEZ. And the menudo, don't forget the menudo.

SILVERS. Oh!! The menudo, we must not forget the menudo. To be a kosher grocer today you have to sell menudo.

MOONEY. Well, like you said Izzie, times is changin' and you got to go with the flow.

SILVERS. *(To Mooney.)* Yes, but menudo? Cow stomach? Come on! Sometimes I think you people would eat shit as long as it was fried in lard.

MOONEY. Don't look at me!! Joe's the tamale man around here!!! (*MOONEY starts getting Mrs. Goldstein's groceries.*)

SILVERS. Black, Mexican, what the hell's the difference. You're all just a bunch of schvarzars to me.

CHAVEZ. Okay, just for you, tonight Lupe and I will eat gefilte fish burritos and smell for a week.

SILVERS. That would be nice, something I can relate to.

MOONEY. You got a box I can put this in?

CHAVEZ. Here's one. (*Handing Silvers two dollars.*) And here's one for yesterday and one for today and my magic number is ...

SILVERS. Ten.

CHAVEZ. What?

SILVERS. Your magic number is ten. It's always ten.

CHAVEZ. How do you know goddamn it! Maybe I changed my mind?

SILVERS. So what is it?

CHAVEZ. My magic number is ... nine.

SILVERS. Nine?

CHAVEZ. Nine.

SILVERS. Nine it is.

CHAVEZ. No wait! I changed my mind. My magic number is ten.

SILVERS. Ten huh? That's a good choice.

MOONEY. Big mistake, Chavez, big mistake.

CHAVEZ. Why? What do you know that I don't? What's going on?

MOONEY. Naw. I keep tellin' you to get here earlier in the morning to gather intelligence.

(PHONE rings.)

CHAVEZ. Aye, cabron! There she is again.

SILVERS. No. It's not. It's Mrs. Cohen.

CHAVEZ. I'll bet you. *(Holds out dollar.)*

SILVERS. Good morning. Silvers' Market. Oh! Good morning Mrs. Cohen. *(Takes dollar.)*

CHAVEZ. How does he do that?

(Starts taking order as MOONEY is packing Mrs. Goldstein's groceries and JAMAR reenters.)

SILVERS. Uh huh ... Uh huh ... He just brought them in, they're still hot ... just a second ... *(To Chavez.)* Did you make the tortillas with lard?

CHAVEZ. No, vegetable oil like you wanted ... kosher.

SILVERS. Funny! If Mexico has Catskills you should go there. He said he used oil, Mrs. Cohen ... Okay, one dozen tortillas. *(Hand over phone.)* Oy vey, Jews eating Mexican. What's this world coming to ... Okay, Mrs. Cohen, we'll have it over there shortly ... Thank you, Mrs. Cohen.

JAMAR. You want me to run that over, Mr. Silvers?

(The MEN look at each other a little puzzled.)

MOONEY. We run the groceries, son.

CHAVEZ. I'll run it over. I promised to fix her storm door.

SILVERS. On the way over there would you drop off Mrs. Anderson's medicine? I picked it up at the drug store on the way to work.

CHAVEZ. I'll go there first.

SILVERS. (*HE hands CHAVEZ a bottle of pills and an apple.*) And give her this, too. Tell her to enjoy. The poor woman.

MOONEY. (*Talking to self while packing groceries.*) And we'll just put this here and that right here.

CHAVEZ. (*Teasing.*) My, you do that so well, amigo. Where did you learn to do that so good, Vo Tech?

MOONEY. (*Chucking.*) No! CETA program.

CHAVEZ. CETA program. (*Laughs.*)

(*City inspector, LENORA KAUFMAN enters. SHE is an overly officious woman, unappreciated and underpaid. SHE is wearing a plastic badge clipped to her pocket and is carrying a clipboard. SHE says nothing as SHE begins to inspect the building.*)

KAUFMAN. Silvers, you really should put some salt on those steps. I could fall and kill myself.

SILVERS. (*Darkened mood.*) Good morning, Mrs. Kaufman.

(*KAUFMAN gives Silvers a quick look. Then inspects Chavez and Mooney and Jamar up and down, gives Silvers a glare, mumbles something inaudible and continues toward the basement stairs.*)

KAUFMAN. Get this light fixed. I could get electrocuted or fall and kill myself. (*SHE takes out flashlight and goes down the basement.*)

SILVERS. (*To self.*) I should be so lucky.

KAUFMAN. (*Peeking around corner.*) What!!

SILVERS. I said you're right, Mrs. Kaufman. I'll replace the light.

CHAVEZ. (*To Silvers.*) What's she doing back? Wasn't she just here?

JAMAR. Who is she?

MOONEY. The electrical inspector.

JAMAR. What's she doing here on a Saturday?

SILVERS. That dame takes her work very seriously.

JAMAR. Schmuck!

(ALL MEN give Jamar a double take.)

SILVERS. Jamar. Why don't you take those boxes down to the basement and kind of keep an eye on what she's doing.

JAMAR. Right. (*Goes to basement stairs with boxes.*)

SILVERS. (*Whisper.*) And don't make it too obvious.

JAMAR. (*Whisper.*) Okay. (*JAMAR exits and loud CRASH is heard. JAMAR has fallen.*)

SILVERS. He's okay, Mooney. The inspector cushioned his fall.

(PHONE rings.)

SILVERS. (*Answers phone. Irritated.*) What?!! ... (*To men.*) What's a four letter word for throw?

(THEY don't know.)

SILVERS. No one knows. Bye, sweetheart. (*Goes to chalk board.*)

MOONEY. I'll be leaving now for Mrs. Goldstein's.

CHAVEZ. Let's see now, it takes five minutes to walk there, two minutes to put the groceries away and after you sit to chat with her ... see you next week.

MOONEY. What?

CHAVEZ. See you next week.

MOONEY. I heard that.

CHAVEZ. You're spending a lot of time over there, Elvis. What do you two talk about for so long?

SILVERS. There isn't that much to talk about to a woman.

MOONEY. Well, we just ...

(PHONE rings.)

SILVERS. *(Answers phone. Beat then to men.)* Hurl, the word is hurl. Thank you, sweetheart. See what I mean?

CHAVEZ. You just what?

MOONEY. She just talks.

CHAVEZ. About what?

MOONEY. About ... you know, things, anything.

CHAVEZ. Personal things?

MOONEY. Well ... yea, we have touched.

SILVERS. Great. Now they're touching. This is getting good.

MOONEY. No We haven't touched! What I was going to say before you interrupted me is that ah ... we ah ... yes! We have talked about some ... kind of ... you might say intimate things ... yes!

CHAVEZ. Intimate!!

(CHAVEZ and SILVERS move in for the kill)

SILVERS. Is this the word I just heard? Intimate?

CHAVEZ. I heard it too, with this ear.

MOONEY. Look, I got to get on my way. Here, fellas. I'd like to discuss this with you further, but I can see that this discussion is gonna end up being the same old trashy bullshit it always ends up being and I got a woman waitin' for me who's hungry.

SILVERS. No, no, no wait. This is getting good, you've never said that word before ... intimate ... you two aren't, you know ...

MOONEY. No! I don't know. We aren't what?

SILVERS. (*Coyly*) I don't know. You tell us.

CHAVEZ. It's okay, Izzie, Doctor Ruth says that this thing happens all the time to senior citizens. It's only normal.

MOONEY. What's normal?

CHAVEZ. You know. To deliver groceries to old women and sit there for twelve hours and watch them try to eat, talk and be intimate at the same time.

SILVERS. That must make you very nervous.

MOONEY. The only thing that makes me nervous is watching how much food that woman packs in her face 'cuz I know it's not good for her ...

SILVERS and CHAVEZ. It's not good, no. No, it s not.

MOONEY. ... makes me feel a little guilty sometimes...

SILVERS. You shouldn't.

MOONEY. ... almost like I was a drug dealer or something.

SILVERS. That you're not.

CHAVEZ. You're not a drug dealer.

MOONEY. ... but it makes her happy and so I guess that makes it alright.

CHAVEZ. Doctor Ruth says that sometimes women eat to hide their ...

SILVERS/CHAVEZ. ... sexual frustrations.

MOONEY. If that were true then as ugly as Doctor Ruth is, she'd weigh twelve hundred pounds.

SILVERS. Mrs. Goldstein hasn't ever ... like ... come on to you?

MOONEY. I'm tellin' ya, nothing like that ever goes on. We just sit and talk 'cuz she likes it.

SILVERS/CHAVEZ. She likes it. Come on, Mooney. There's more to this. Give us the gory details.

MOONEY. (*Gives the locker room boys what they want to hear.*) All right, okay, okay. The only thing that ever happened is once I caught her looking at my butt. Okay! You feel better now?

(*SILVERS and CHAVEZ try to contain themselves as CHAVEZ peeks under Mooney's coat.*)

CHAVEZ. Well, who could blame her? You have such a cute one. Look, Izzie, doesn't Elvis have a cute butt?

SILVERS. Butts? Butts? What's a butt? I don't have one. Chavez, what's a butt?

CHAVEZ. I don't know, I can't remember. I think I used to have one. Oh, yea! Now I remember. Mine was so cute and cuddly. It used to follow me around wherever I went.

SILVERS. You called him Fido.

CHAVEZ. His bark was worse than his bite.

SILVERS. Well, his voice has changed but his breath is still the same.

(BOTH MEN are on the floor.)

MOONEY. See how you guys are, can never be serious. Got to always be making a joke out of everything.

CHAVEZ. Who's joking, Mooney? I would gladly deliver Mrs. Goldstein's groceries ... if I had a butt.

(CHAVEZ and SILVERS crack up.)

MOONEY. Oh man, I see!

CHAVEZ. Come on, Mooney! We're just giving you a hard time, amigo ... besides she's really not a bad looking ole gal.

MOONEY. I'm glad you noticed that. I think so, too.

SILVERS. Yes, indeed! When she's not talking and those chins aren't shaking she has a certain charm about her.

MOONEY. All right. That's enough, children. You guys just won't let go of it will you ... besides, when it comes to what you guys are talking about, I like my women younger.

SILVERS. Oh? How young is that?

MOONEY. Late twenties, early thirties.

SILVERS. Schmuck. At your age you couldn't handle a woman that young.

MOONEY. You wanna bet? I may be old and it may take me a while to get the ole engine revved up but once I do, I throw it into first gear, then it's just a matter of time before I kick into overdrive. It's in the genes.

CHAVEZ. Not me. My battery is run down and I lost my jumper cables a long time ago.

SILVERS. Amen to that. I'll tell you this Mooney, you'd better stick to someone your own age or make sure she's a nurse.

MOONEY. Why? What can a nurse do for me that another woman can't?

SILVERS. CPR!

MOONEY. I can't hear a damn word you guys are saying ... too old, remember? (*Begins to leave.*) It's in the genes boys, it's in the genes.

SILVERS. Yea! Well, make sure you stay out of her jeans. It could be bad for business. Go! Go, get out of here and take your butt with you, you show off.

CHAVEZ. Maybe it would be good for business, you know, like in those T.V. commercials? Are you old, lonely and hungry? Just go to your phone and call 1-900 Dial-a-Deliman. Callers, get permission from your parents first, if they're still alive.

SILVERS. (*Shaking head in disgust.*) I've known you fifty years Chavez, and you're still a sick man. (*Pauses.*) Do you think anyone would call?

CHAVEZ. Yes.

CHAVEZ/SILVERS. Mrs. Goldstein.

CHAVEZ. You know, one of these days, he's going to haul off and hit us.

SILVERS. Did we go too far with Elvis this time?

CHAVEZ. Maybe a little. Something's different about him and her lately. I don't know if it worries me or makes me happy for him.

SILVERS. He used to kid about her, too.

CHAVEZ. That man there is as lonely as she is. When Betty died, he was crushed, wasn't the same. Started drinking.

SILVERS. It was a hard road back for him. And it was a hard road back for Mrs. Goldstein, too. She's been through a lot.

CHAVEZ. You see, we forget how lucky we are. I have Lupe. You have Milley. He has no one, except her and this store.

SILVERS. It scares me sometimes, Joe, to think of what this life would be like without Milley.

(PHONE.)

SILVERS. *(Answers.)* What now? ... Bob Barker is very old ... bye, sweetheart. *(Hangs up. Chalks up.)* She drives me crazy.

CHAVEZ. Well, I might as well get Mrs. Cohen's order on its way.

(CHAVEZ starts to put order together as JAMAR comes upstairs.)

CHAVEZ. Well, Gordon Lightfoot, what's going on down there?

JAMAR. I don't know. She just kept pokin' around down there and jabbering to herself.

CHAVEZ. She's taking a long time down there.

SILVERS. I was just thinking the same thing. *(Pause.)* This is the third time she's been here in the last two months.

CHAVEZ What does she say?

SILVERS. Fix this, fix that, nothing big but a lot of little things. She started coming around a lot about the same time all that talk was going on about the city building more low income housing.

CHAVEZ. What time? It hasn't stopped. The city has been talking about and building low income housing on the Northside for years. It's a joke.

SILVERS. Tell me about jokes.

CHAVEZ. They tear down good houses where low income people live in the first place then they built this cheap shit that falls apart and looks like hell. Then they stand there and say, "Oh, those people over there. They just don't know how to take care of things."

SILVERS. This is what I'm saying.

CHAVEZ. Then you read in the paper and see on television about all the crime on the Northside and they think the answer is more police. More witness to our misery. The answer is to give the people the means to live in a place they can be proud of.

JAMAR. How can you do that?

CHAVEZ. Money, jobs, loans. Let the people have some of the money we spend on these goddamn wars. Put it in their hands, don't spend it *for* them, for what you *think* they need.

JAMAR. I can dig that.

CHAVEZ. And as far as crime? You can't have people living one on top of each other, shoulder to shoulder.

JAMAR. The kids with no yards to play in.

CHAVEZ. No, you can't have that and not expect trouble.

SILVERS. You treat a man like a child. He'll act like a child.

CHAVEZ. Where were the witnesses in the '50s? Where was the media when the city committed the worst crime of all and threw us crumbs and turned their backs while the heart of our community was torn out?

SILVERS. I'll tell you where they were. They were living in the suburbs next door to all those other do-gooders who were planning our future in the name of progress.

CHAVEZ. Progress my ass!! They were just trying to figure out what part of our neighborhood to tear down to build another goddamn freeway.

JAMAR. Yea! So they could get home faster!

CHAVEZ. When I think of what we lost it pisses me off.

JAMAR. It pisses me off too and I wasn't even born yet! Come on, let's go kick this inspector's ass!!!! (*JAMAR moves for basement and takes old men by surprise.*)

CHAVEZ/SILVERS. Hey, hey, slow down, son. Chill out.

(*THEY sit JAMAR down, amusing him by this sudden attention.*)

SILVERS. What were they thinking of? This was such a wonderful place to live, so alive. Jamar, you should have seen it.

(*The OLD MEN reminisce for themselves but also to pass on the memories, the legacy, to Jamar.*)

CHAVEZ. Ted Bussy's Bait Store and the Brynwood Theater on Glenwood Avenue, Sumner School and all the little shops along Olson Highway.

JAMAR. Shops along Olson Highway?

CHAVEZ. Oh, yea! Lots of 'em. What about Moys Cafe and Western Auto on Broadway?

SILVERS. The Northside Picnic at North Common and the Northside Bakery and Desnik's Drug on Plymouth.

JAMAR. Was the McDonald's there then?

SILVERS/CHAVEZ. No.

JAMAR. Well, they closed it, so it's not there again.

SILVERS/CHAVEZ. Really!

SILVERS. Oh! And up the street at the Homewood Theater, for twenty cents, you could get a box of popcorn and watch a Jeff Chandler double feature.

CHAVEZ. (*Sarcastically.*) Jeff Chandler. Whoopee.

JAMAR. Boring huh?

CHAVEZ. Capital punishment.

SILVERS. Jeff Chandler was not boring.

CHAVEZ. Jamar, watching Jeff Chandler was like sitting through a Barry Manilow concert.

JAMAR. (*Grossed out.*) Ugh!

SILVERS. Jeff Chandler was not boring. It was in the days of censorship and they wouldn't let him cut loose. He was a time bomb waiting to happen.

CHAVEZ. Remember going to Skip's Barbecue over by Greenstein's Market after the movies? Old Pumpkin Joe made sure every kid in the neighborhood had a pumpkin for Halloween.

SILVERS. St. Joseph's Church and ... (*Beat.*) Joe, I'm sorry.

(Pause.)

CHAVEZ. Losing our church ... That hurt the most, amigo. It killed the Northside for me. It was the center of our lives ... we baptized our children there and sent them to school there ... when Carlos died, we said goodbye there and since there was no body ... when they took the church, it was like they took away my boy again.

SILVERS. I remember when you and Lupe were married there.

CHAVEZ. What a day that was. Remember the party after?

SILVERS. How could I forget?

CHAVEZ. How could you remember?

SILVERS. Please, you'll give the boy a bad idea of me.

CHAVEZ. Jews and Tequila don't mix. When you got sick in the back yard next to the garage, you looked like a rabbi at the Wailing Wall.

JAMAR. Cold.

SILVERS. You know, Joe, time has gone by so fast. Sometimes when a jet goes overhead, I close my eyes and I don't hear a jet. I hear a big yellow street car rumbling past the front of the store. That's it! It's the sounds of the old Northside that I miss most ... the clakity clak of the ragman's horse, the sound of a sputtering '36 Ford, the music the factory whistles made at quitting time at Munsingwear. (*BOTH make factory whistle sound.*) It's time to go home to your families!! Get your lunch buckets and go home to your families!!

CHAVEZ. The banging of the boxcars in the yards and the big locomotives trying to get the train moving. What were those called?

SILVERS. Yellowstones!

CHAVEZ. Yea, yellowstones. (*Imitates locomotive.*) Chug ... chug ... chugga, chugga, chugga, chugga, chugga.

SILVERS. Remember all the racket the coal man used to make? When he would deliver coal to your house, you didn't have to watch to know what was going on. You would hear the loud clink and thud of him opening the steel coal door on the side of the house, the squeak of the metal chute that he pulled from the side of his truck, then the humming of the truck as he tilted it back, to dump the coal. Then that loud rushing of coal sliding down into the basement. Then when it stopped, there was always that last few tink tinks of the last bits of coal.

CHAVEZ. You'll never hear those sounds Jamar, and that's too bad.

SILVERS. It's almost like someone felt that the old neighborhood was too nice for us. Projects! Build more projects, remind the people they're poor.

CHAVEZ. But even living in the projects back then was different. It had a sense of respect. There was hope for better things. You could be poor with dignity ... that was our community's biggest loss, it's dignity. And it's not just the people downtown I blame, Izzie. It's us.

JAMAR. How can you blame yourselves?

CHAVEZ. Because, we let them do it. We sat back and let it happen. We didn't fight. We trusted them and they stole our history.

SILVERS. History, what history? The poor don't have a history. They're born, they struggle, they die, then they're forgotten. It wouldn't have made any difference, Joe. The poor people have never had a voice in this. We were left to just pick up the pieces.

CHAVEZ. Well, it's not right. (*Long pause as HE looks out the window.*) You know, it's kind of funny to hear you talk of yourself as being poor. I remember being envious of you, thinking of you as just another rich Judio.

SILVERS. (*Laughs.*) You and a lot of other people. It's been hand to mouth, Joe, hand to mouth.

CHAVEZ. I know it has, Izzie, I remember, I know, I know.

SILVERS. Ah, ah, ah, stop with the I knows already.

CHAVEZ. You've been a good amigo, amigo ... I remember that first summer when I decided to stop working the fields and settle here on the Northside and you gave me credit when no one else would.

SILVERS. I remember you going down to Farmer's Market every morning before work and buying vegetables for us when I was in the hospital.

CHAVEZ. (*Laughs.*) It beat picking 'em. Besides, I was proud of that. You were the king of the kosher grocers. Everyone knew Izzie Silvers and I was your buyer. It made me feel important.

SILVERS. (*Solemn.*) King of the kosher grocers ... business was good then ... now look. The deli case is full of junk food and mineral water and we're running a lonely hearts club. Next thing you know I'll be open twenty-four hours and selling lottery tickets.

(*Enter KAUFMAN. SHE walks up to the counter gives Silvers a little smirk and begins to write.*)

SILVERS. Well?

*(KAUFMAN continues writing. There is a long pause as
    SILVERS and CHAVEZ watch her. JAMAR looks
    over Kaufman's shoulder which irritates her.)*

JAMAR. *(Jokingly.)* You're going to get writer's
cramp.
SILVERS. *(To Jamar.)* Shhhh ... what are you writing?
CHAVEZ. Get over here, son. This is none of our
concern.

*(CHAVEZ and JAMAR step away but stay in hearing
    distance.)*

KAUFMAN. I told you the last time I was here, Mr.
Silvers.
SILVERS. Told me what?
KAUFMAN. About the electrical repairs in the
basement.
SILVERS. But I repaired the wiring and the plumbing
... well, the plumbing? I got bids and I'll have to get more
bids because the ones I got are too high ...
KAUFMAN. Plumbing is not my department. As far as
the wiring, you'll have to do it again.
SILVERS. Do it again!!!!
KAUFMAN. Yea, do it again. It doesn't meet code,
plus you never got a permit. *(Continues writing.)* You
should be able to get everything done for under a thou ...
SILVERS. A thousand! It might as well be a million!
JAMAR. You're wrong man, that's wrong.
SILVERS. Jamar, keep quiet.

*(KAUFMAN finishes writing and gives to Silvers to sign.
SILVERS signs, SHE signs and tears off copy and
gives to Silvers.)*

SILVERS. When does it have to be done?

KAUFMAN. Thirty days.

SILVERS. Thirty days!! I can't have it all done in thirty days. I'll need more time than that!!!

KAUFMAN. You have thirty days.

SILVERS. Or what happens?

KAUFMAN. You'll be fined or we could close you ... or both.

SILVERS. You close me? That's it? That simple? After fifty years, you just close me?

KAUFMAN. Yes, it's that simple.

SILVERS. You can't do this.

KAUFMAN. No? It's done. It's out of my hands now.

SILVERS. So whose hands is it in?

KAUFMAN. My supervisor, your alderman, the city council, the taxpayers, the city of Minneapolis. Take your pick. But I'll tell you one thing, the bottom line is, if these repairs aren't completed in thirty days, it could be in the hands of the sheriff's department.

SILVERS. (*Explodes.*) The sheriff's department!!? What am I? A criminal? I may have voted for Nixon but I am not a crook!!!

KAUFMAN. It's the law, Silvers. It's the law.

SILVERS. Does the law have no compassion? ... No! This is my store, you're standing in my store!! Get the hell out of here!!!

KAUFMAN. Okay, Silvers, you wanna play hard ball. I'm gonna have the goddamn building, plumbing, heating, sidewalk, and any other damn city inspector I can find in city hall, come down here and pay you a visit, too.

(KAUFMAN exits, slamming the front door. SILVERS stands in stunned silence. CHAVEZ starts to bag Mrs. Cohen's groceries, SILVERS gathers self and still confused, tries to find something to do but stops and stares at the door. CHAVEZ picks up bag and heads for the door.)

SILVERS. I shouldn't have let myself get so upset.

JAMAR. She just wanted you to kiss her ass.

SILVERS. I wish I would have.

JAMAR. Never kiss nobody's ass.

SILVERS. Jamar, when a man puts his whole life into something in order to survive, it's not called kissing ass. It's called good business.

(Pause.)

JAMAR. I mean, who in the hell does she think she is?

CHAVEZ. I'll tell you who she is, she's just a little person with a little power, a nobody. She can't close you down!

SILVERS. I'm afraid she can. She's got the law on her side so that makes her a big person with a lot of power.

CHAVEZ. Well ... *(HE is lost for words.)*

SILVERS. *(Still fixed on door.)* You asked how it happened, Joe? This is how it happened. This is how they destroyed the old neighborhood. It started with one frayed wire or a rotten board. When they think you've outlived your privileges and it's time for you to leave, this is how they do it. The destruction of the whole Northside probably started with one leaky pipe.

CHAVEZ. No!! They can't close you. Don't they know who you are? You're the king of the kosher grocers. (*Pause.*) Right?

SILVERS. (*Pause, then tenderly.*) Right.

CHAVEZ. (*Quietly.*) I'm going to Mrs. Cohen's now. (*Pause.*) I'll be right back. You won't be alone. Jamar's here. (*Long pause.*) Do you want me to pick you up something from the store?

SILVERS. This is a store.

CHAVEZ. Yea, but you always eat the food here. I just thought as a special treat I could pick you up something from a different store, maybe some Twinkies?

SILVERS. (*Still dazed.*) Some Ho Ho's would be nice.

(*Long pause as CHAVEZ quietly leaves.*)

JAMAR. What are we going to do? (*Pause.*) Mr. Silvers, what are we going to do?

SILVERS. What are we going to do? (*Suddenly snaps out of it.*) I tell you what we're going to do. We are going to go back to work, that's what we're going to do. (*PHONE begins ringing.*) Jamar, bring up that case of Bud Light from the beer cooler ... (*Answers the phone brightly.*) Silvers' Market ... Oh! Good morning, Mrs. Gustufson. How are you today? ... I couldn't be better, thank you! How's Mr. Gustufson ... I know ... I know ... I know.

(*As LIGHTS fade to BLACK.*)

ACT II

It is early morning at Silvers' Market. We hear the PHONE ring three times. The post intermission LIGHTS fade and loud pumpin' RAP MUSIC blares from the newly set boom box on the counter. LIGHTS snap on to reveal JAMAR coming up from the basement with a box of groceries to stock, dancing while restocking the shelves. JAMAR notices a figure in the window coming to the store. HE crosses to the door to unlock and greet his best friend, BILLY MOSS. BILLY is an Afro-American man in his early 20s. HE wears a Raiders starter jacket, Black Sox basement cap, jeans, Air Jordans, and has his Walkman headphones wrapped around his neck. His coat is buttoned.

BILLY. (*Listening to music.*) Uh-oh, this is the cut!

(JAMAR crosses back to register and places bills and coins in the till. BILLY begins rapping and dancing to the song as HE crosses the stage. He high-fives JAMAR. JAMAR takes over the rap while BILLY dances. In the instrumental, the TWO execute a choreographed combination. At the end of the dance, JAMAR turns down radio.)

BILLY. Yo man, what you gotta do that for? I was just gettin' funky.

(BILLY opens his jacket to reveal a large clock he wears from a chain around his neck. HE crosses to Jamar, THEY greet in a choreographed series of slaps, shakes and gestures. It's their ritual greeting.)

BILLY. Yo, Jamar!

JAMAR. Yo, Billy.

BILLY. Yo. You got some salt for the sidewalk? Some old motherfucker's gonna fall and break their ass.

JAMAR. Damn, I forgot. Behind the door, homes.

BILLY. Yea, cuz those old motherfucks will sue immediately, know what I'm sayin'?

(BILLY grabs bag and quickly salts down sidewalk as PHONE rings. JAMAR studies it and looks at watch.)

JAMAR. Good morning, Mrs. Goldstein ... Oh? *(Wrong guess.)* Sorry, Mrs. Zimmerman. Can I take your order? ... Okay ... Uh huh ...

(BILLY reenters as JAMAR continues taking order.)

BILLY. Yo, home.

JAMAR. *(Stops him with raised hand.)* Yea, okay ... okay, Mrs. Zimmerman, say when did you want this delivered? ... Oh wow, I'm alone and I ... well, just a second ... Eh, Billy, can you do me a favor and run an order for me?

BILLY. Funny you should ask for a favor, I was ...

JAMAR. Come on man, the lady's waiting!

BILLY. It's done, homes.

JAMAR. Mrs. Zimmerman, my friend, Billy Moss, will run it right over for you ... the side door ... right ... okay, bye, Mrs. Zimmerman ... (*Finishes writing up order and begins to put order together.*)

BILLY. Jamar, check it out, we got this gig in Rochester ...

JAMAR. And your band needs my van again, right?

BILLY. Right.

JAMAR. What about Ricco's van?

BILLY. Man, that thing ain't going to make it there and back. Come on man, I'll take care of it, I'll have it back to you, boom, Monday morning.

JAMAR. Yea, that's what you said the last time. Got my van back a day late, no gas, smelled all funky 'n shit.

(*PHONE rings. JAMAR guesses again.*)

JAMAR. Mrs. Silvers.

BILLY. Yea, right.

JAMAR. (*Answers.*) Good morning, Silvers' Market ... (*Bingo.*) Oh, hello, Mrs. Silvers.

BILLY. Lucky guess.

JAMAR. No, he isn't back yet ... oh, I'm sorry. I must have been in the basement when you called ... Okay, I'll tell him ... Okay ... Good bye, Mrs. Silvers.

BILLY. Come on, man. Where you got to go this weekend? Why don't you cruise up there with us?

JAMAR. No. I can't go with you man. I'm giving the old man a hand here for a while.

BILLY. I promise, homes. (*Sits in Mooney's chair.*)

JAMAR. Let me think about it. Better not sit there.

BILLY. Yea, right. (*Does not move.*)

(MOONEY enters store, looks back at sidewalk looks at bag of rock salt on wrong side of door and puts it on the other side. Gives Jamar disapproving look over rap music playing.)

JAMAR. Morning, Grandpa. *(JAMAR goes to change to music his Grandpa would like.)*

MOONEY. Hey! Jamar. *(Stops dead in his tracks. BILLY is sitting in his chair.)*

BILLY. Oh, Mr. Mooney. *(Feeling the glare.)* What? Oh. *(Understands and moves to Chavez's chair.)*

JAMAR. Told ya.

(The glare remains.)

BILLY. Not this one either, huh? *(BILLY gets up and moves away.)*

MOONEY. Hey, Billy. *(Looks at watch.)* Mrs. Goldstein called her order in yet?

JAMAR. No, not yet. Here, Billy, run this over to Mrs. Zimmerman's.

MOONEY. She's late. *(Going to chalkboard.)* Mrs. Silvers called?

JAMAR. She lives at 811 Humboldt. Go to the side door.

MOONEY. Did Mrs. Silvers call?

JAMAR. *(A little bothered by his Grandpa's interruptions.)* Just a second, Grandpa. Go to the side door and after you knock, step back so she can see who you ... *(Takes a look at Billy.)* On second thought, stand close to the door so she can't see you.

BILLY. Oh, man, that's ill.

JAMAR. Don't forget to get the money.

BILLY. Yea, all right. Later. (*HE leaves.*)

JAMAR. Yea, she called, Grandpa.

MOONEY. You didn't mark it up? How many times she call?

JAMAR. I dunno, I was in the basement.

MOONEY. Damn, Jamar! Well, let's just say it was three. (*MOONEY tallies three calls.*) What are you doing here today, Jamar? Thought you just worked Saturday mornings. How come you ain't in school?

JAMAR. Mr. Silvers called me last night and asked me to open for him today. He said he wasn't feeling too good and he wanted to go see Doc Eisenstat this morning. I don't know, Gramps. I stopped in yesterday and he wasn't looking too good.

MOONEY. I understand your concern, son, but what about school? You can't be missing any school.

JAMAR. (*Guilty.*) Grandpa. I wanted to talk to you about that.

MOONEY. Boy, you can't be missing any school. You got to get that degree and make something out of yourself. Your mama's been working hard to pay for your schooling so you can make a good life for yourself. Good Lord!

JAMAR. (*Ready to confess.*) Gramps.

MOONEY. You been missing a lot of school?

(*JAMAR is silent.*)

MOONEY. I fear for you son, that's all. I don't want you to end up in the streets like a lot of the kids around here. Selling drugs, flipping hamburgers. You got to get that degree.

JAMAR. Hum!! A lot of good a degree is going to do me.

MOONEY. What do you mean?

JAMAR. What I want is to own my own business some day, you know? Be my own boss. But degree or no degree, ain't no bank gonna loan money to some Northside nigger with a dream.

MOONEY. They ain't going to give money to nobody with an attitude like that, especially a Northside nigger with a bad attitude.

CHAVEZ. (*Enter CHAVEZ with tortillas and HE is in high spirits.*) Who's got a bad attitude? Not me! It' s a beautiful day, it's a wonderful day. Nothing could be better.

MOONEY. Who lit a fire under you, amigo?

CHAVEZ. Lupe.

MOONEY. Lupe?

CHAVEZ. You remember when I said my batteries was run down? Well, last night, I found my jumper cables.

MOONEY. (*Impressed.*) Why you old sly son of a bitch. How was it?

CHAVEZ. (*Beat.*) I can't remember. Hey, how come you're not in school?

JAMAR. (*Frustrated but being precise.*) Mr. Silvers called me last night and asked me to come in and open for him because he wasn't feeling good, so I said okay because when I came in yesterday, he wasn't looking very well and ... oh, forget it! Gramps, we'll talk about it later.

MOONEY. Well, okay, but if Izzie calls you again, you let your ole Grandpa Elvis and the Mexican here take care of things around here.

JAMAR. Promise.

CHAVEZ. I think all this pressure's getting to him.

JAMAR. It's no wonder. The way them damn city inspectors been giving him such a hard time.

MOONEY. Izzie and Chavez think it's some sort of, what did you call it?

CHAVEZ. Conspiracy.

JAMAR. A conspiracy? Is that what you think, Gramps?

MOONEY. I don't know. But I do know that that inspector's a peckerwood.

CHAVEZ. It's a conspiracy! Those pinche ...? ... schmuccas ...?

(To JAMAR and MOONEY that last word didn't quite sound right.)

JAMAR. Well, I hate to say it but they do have a point.

(MOONEY and CHAVEZ are taken back.)

MOONEY. What you sayin', boy?

JAMAR. Well, this place is getting pretty run down. I mean, none of the coolers in the basement are working, half of the display racks are broken, the ceiling tiles are falling down.

MOONEY. The business is tired, son.

JAMAR. Yes, but it makes business worse when people come in here and it's so run down. How come he doesn't fix it up?

CHAVEZ. It takes money, hombre.

JAMAR. Well, I know business hasn't been that great but he must have some money tucked away. From what you two say, this place used to be a gold mine.

MOONEY. Well, I don't know about a gold mine. Izzie used to do a pretty good business but I can tell you that he hasn't got much tucked away.

CHAVEZ. What little he had put away went for doctor bills when Milley took sick the last time.

MOONEY. No, Izzie ain't got much put away anymore, I know that for a fact. (*Looks at watch as HE goes for coffee but Chavez has taken the last of it.*) Damn! When's that woman going to call? Out of coffee already?

JAMAR. Didn't make any. That was left over from yesterday.

(*CHAVEZ with a mouthful of old coffee is grossed out and spits it back into his cup.*)

MOONEY. (*A little disappointed.*) Jamar.

CHAVEZ. I'll put it on.

JAMAR. You drink too much coffee anyway, Grandpa.

MOONEY. Now, you just never mind about how much coffee your old granddaddy drinks. If you want to worry about something, think about the brain damage you're getting listening to that damn rap music. Music!! Hell, that ain't music!! You ain't never heard music till you heard Count Basie, the Mills Brothers, now that was music. (*Starts to sing a popular 40s romantic ballad.*)

CHAVEZ. (*Covering ears.*) Oh no! Not Mrs. Goldstein's favorite song again!!!

MOONEY. Don't start in on me, Chavez.

CHAVEZ. Quick, Jamar, put on some Two Live Crew.

(PHONE rings.)

MOONEY. Mrs. Goldstein. *(Relieved.)*

JAMAR. Bet it is. Good morning, Silvers' Market ... No, Mr. Silvers isn't here, this is Jamar ...

MOONEY. Tell that girl she ought to be ashamed of herself for oversleeping. *(Laughs.)*

CHAVEZ. Ask her if she dreamt of Mooney.

JAMAR. ... yea, he's right here ma'am, just a second ... Grandpa, it's for you.

(Hands MOONEY the phone. Long beat.)

MOONEY. Hello? This is Elvis ... Well, hello, Mrs. Copstein. It's nice to hear your voice. You callin' from Chicago? ... All the guys wanted to ... *(MOONEY turns to stone.)*

CHAVEZ. Ask her how come she didn't stop by ...

(MOONEY sets down phone on counter and sits.)

CHAVEZ. Amigo, what's wrong? *(Picks up phone.)* Hello?

JAMAR. Grandpa? .... What is it? What's wrong?

CHAVEZ. No, Karen, this is Joe. Is there something wrong with your mama? ... I see ... I see ... Okay ... Okay, honey, I'll tell Izzie ... Are you going to be okay? ... Okay, bye ... Yes, yes. We love you too, Karen, bye. *(Hangs up phone. CHAVEZ is stunned.)* Jamar, that was Mrs. Goldstein's daughter. She said, she said that, that Mrs. Goldstein passed away this morning.

JAMAR. Damn!

CHAVEZ. She just got the call from Doc Eisenstat. He told her Mrs. Goldstein was havin' chest pains early this morning and called 911. He said when they got there, it was too late. She was already gone.

CHAVEZ. (*Takes seat next to the stunned MOONEY.*) Pobrecita.

JAMAR. Gramps ...

(*MOONEY, elbows on knees, hands together in prayer, eyes closed, shakes his head slowly. This isn't happening to him again.*)

CHAVEZ. (*Suddenly feeling guilty about the kidding.*) Elvis ... I ... the way we joke about her here ... we ...

JAMAR. It's okay, Mr. Chavez, Grandpa knows better. He knows where you're kidding comes from.

CHAVEZ. Yes, but ...

MOONEY. When my Betty died ... when my Betty died ... I ah, took it kind of bad, felt pretty bad. I ah, kind of checked out for a while, needed to be alone. I remember I didn't cry, just got mad, got real mad at everything. Cursed God. Got mad at Betty for dying, even got mad at myself for falling in love with the woman in the first place. Walking around just being angry all the time because I was afraid of ... missing my lady. When you and Izzie came and dragged me out of the house and back down here, well, then some of that madness started leaving me and that loneliness took over. Traded one misery for another. Mrs. Goldstein never took that sorrow away from me but the sound of her voice eased the pain. (*Pause.*) I can't figure it out, but there's something about a woman's voice that can ease a man's pain. Don't know what it is, but a woman's voice is almost like a, like a warm blanket wrapped around you when it's cold out ... I'm gonna miss that lady.

(BELL over door signals SILVERS' arrival. HE doesn't look well. HE stops at door and knows what's going on.)

JAMAR. Morning, Mr. Silvers.

SILVERS. Morning, Jamar. (*Pause.*) I see you've already heard.

CHAVEZ. Yes, just a few minutes ago. Her daughter called. (*Goes to Mooney and pats shoulder.*)

MOONEY. Thanks, Izzie. I appreciate that.

SILVERS. What a terrible, terrible thing. She was such a nice old woman. Doctor Eisenstat broke the news to me at the clinic. I'm sick about it, just sick.

(PHONE.)

SILVERS. Hello, sweetheart ... yes, we know ... I'm fine ... I love you too, bye. (*Hangs up.*) Thanks, Jamar, I appreciate you coming in today and giving me a hand. Sorry you had to miss school today.

JAMAR. No problem, Mr. Silvers.

CHAVEZ. Well?

SILVERS. Well, what?

CHAVEZ. What did the doctor say? He said it was your heart again, didn't he?

SILVERS. No!

CHAVEZ. Goddamn it, Izzie. How many times do we have to tell you to take care of yourself?

SILVERS. No, he didn't say it was my heart.

CHAVEZ. Well, then why did you go into see him?

SILVERS. I was having pains in my rectum.

CHAVEZ. Pains in your rectum? Since when did you start having pains in your rectum?

SILVERS. Since I met you!! (*HE starts to laugh but gets shooting pain in chest.*)

JAMAR. Mr. Silvers, are you all right? (*Goes to grab him.*)

SILVERS. I'm fine. I just have to sit down.

(*All the MEN help him sit, JAMAR goes for water, SILVERS takes out pills.*)

CHAVEZ. Izzie, you need to get off your feet.

SILVERS. Okay, I'll just sit here for awhile.

CHAVEZ. You need some time off, amigo.

SILVERS. Now you sound like Doctor Eisenstat.

MOONEY. Damn it, Silvers! I don't need to go to two funerals.

(*JAMAR returns with water. SILVERS takes pills.*)

CHAVEZ. What exactly did he tell you?

SILVERS. (*Pause.*) He said ... he said I have something wrong. Goddamn it!! Don't understand doctors. They talk like they write!! (*Calms down but is concerned.*) I have some blockage, he wants me to go into the hospital for a few days.

MOONEY. Sounds like more than a few days to me.

CHAVEZ. Then you better do it.

SILVERS. Now how in the hell am I going to do that? What about the store? Who's going to watch the store? Milley can't.

MOONEY. Chavez and me can watch the store.

SILVERS. Neither of you know the first thing about running this store.

CHAVEZ. The hell!!

SILVERS. Sure, you know all of our customers, but what about paying the bills and ordering? No! Thanks, but no thanks. I'd come back and this place would be a mess.

(THEY all look around at the mess.)

SILVERS. Okay, a bigger mess.

JAMAR. I could run the store, Mr. Silvers.

ALL. No, you've got school, you can't miss school.

JAMAR. Yes, I can ... I'm not going to school anymore.

ALL. (*All MEN bolt upright.*) What!!!!!

MOONEY. What you say, boy?

JAMAR. I said I quit.

SILVERS. It's my fault, I shouldn't have called you last night and asked you to open the store.

JAMAR. I've been out of school for a month.

MOONEY. A month!!

SILVERS. But why, son? You know how hard it is to make it without some college.

JAMAR. I wasn't learning anything. I can't learn from books, I got to be doing something.

MOONEY. But what about all your plans, boy?

JAMAR. Right now, my plans don't include school.

MOONEY. Well, of all the ... I don't understand this, I just don't understand kids anymore. Do you know what you're saying? You're saying that you're going to throw away any chance of making anything out of yourself.

SILVERS. Mooney, you're still upset over Mrs. Goldstein. Maybe you should wait and talk ...

MOONEY. Where you been, boy? Hasn't anything sunk into your head?

CHAVEZ. Izzie's right. Maybe ...

MOONEY. I'm talking to my grandson, goddamn it!!!! Your mama and I have worked all our lives to make things better for you, to give you the opportunity to make a better life for yourself. And now when you got it right there for the grabbin' you don't want to take it. I don't know how many times you and I sat and talked about your future. Didn't that mean anything to you?

JAMAR. It meant a lot to me, Grandpa.

MOONEY. Boy, you should be ashamed of yourself!!! Think of all those black folk who've come and gone who grew up in the South who never had a pot to piss in. Do you think they ever had a chance to even think about school?

JAMAR. Right now, I just can't think about that, Grandpa.

MOONEY. Why? You think you're better than them? You better go take a good long look in the mirror, boy. You're just as black as they are. Just born in better times is all. Minnesota is heaven compared to all that misery.

JAMAR. I think it's time you took a long look at me too, Grandpa. I've grown up. I'm a man, I'm not a boy anymore. I said I can't think of those things my people went through when it comes to my future. I respect the suffering but I don't want to chance using it as an excuse. My future is mine and I don't want anything getting in my way of doing what I have to do. And as far as Minnesota being heaven, Gramps? It may be for you, but you ask any kid in the hood where heaven is and they won't know. But you ask them about hell and they'll tell you it starts this side of Plymouth Avenue.

MOONEY. And what about your mama?

JAMAR. That's the other thing, Gramps. I can't see Mama giving me everything she makes anymore. She's startin' to look like an old lady, while I just go to school. Well, I can't take anymore money from her. I need to make my own way and Mama understands.

(All MEN are shocked into silence. MOONEY slowly walks toward door, heartbroken, angry, confused.)

MOONEY. Go head, Izzie, let him help you out. You need the help. It'll keep him off the streets. I got a funeral to get ready for.

JAMAR. Grandpa!

(MOONEY waves him off and leaves.)

CHAVEZ. Compadre! Compadre! He'll be all right, Jamar. He'll get over it.

SILVERS. Yes, Chavez and I will talk to him. (*Pause.*) So you think you can handle things around here for a few days?

CHAVEZ. I'll be around.

SILVERS. That's what I'm afraid of. (*Laughs.*)

(No one else laughs. PHONE rings.)

SILVERS. Yes, sweetheart? ... The blue suit will be fine. No flowers. No, groceries would not be appropriate ... Bye, sweetheart. *(Hangs up.)* Oy vey! What next?

(Enter LENORA KAUFMAN and her supervisor, EARL LEWIS. LEWIS is a 50-ish man, heavyset and mean looking and quiet. HE is dressed in a dark suit, old trench coat with a white shirt open at the collar. HE also is wearing a plastic badge. LEWIS hangs back as KAUFMAN approaches the three.)

KAUFMAN. This is Earl Lewis ... head of inspections. Earl Lewis? *(KAUFMAN is enjoying the whole thing. Starts for basement stairs.)* The basement's over here, Earl.

LEWIS Just a second. Morning, gentlemen. I understand we have some problems to address here. Mrs. Kaufman and some of the other inspectors filed their inspection reports with me and they note quite a few violations.

KAUFMAN. The basement stairs are over here.

LEWIS. I said just a moment.

(KAUFMAN is perturbed.)

LEWIS. As I was saying, the inspectors have noted quite a few violations and ah ... well, I'm going to have to take a closer look around and make a determination ... and then we'll discuss the severity of the violations and what you want to do about them.

SILVERS. Mr. Lewis. I've been here for fifty years and in all those years, I have never been treated ...

LEWIS. Please, Mr. Silvers. I'll discuss this with you later. Now, if you'll excuse me.

(HE starts for basement stairs. KAUFMAN is standing there beaming.)

KAUFMAN. Watch your step. I almost fell and killed myself.

LEWIS. That would have been too bad.

SILVERS. They're going to close me Joe. I know it ... after fifty years in business, they're going to close me.

JAMAR. But they know you can't get everything done all at once.

CHAVEZ. It's a conspiracy.

BILLY. *(Explodes in.)* Yo, yo, yo, Billy's in the house bringin' the funkiest of the funk masters.

(BILLY crosses to till.)

JAMAR. Hey, Billy.

(Both old MEN stare trying to figure out what just walked in.)

BILLY. Boomp! Boomp! Bamm!! *(Puts money in Silvers' hand.)* It's done!!

SILVERS. Can I help you? What's this?

BILLY. Mrs. Zimmerman's grocery money.

JAMAR. He delivered Mrs. Zimmerman's groceries. You remember Billy, Mr. Silvers.

BILLY. (*Striking pose.*) Pow!!

SILVERS. Billy Moss? Manny and Catrice's Billy?

BILLY. The same.

SILVERS. (*To Chavez.*) You remember Billy.

CHAVEZ. Of course. I didn't recognize you. What happened to your hair?

SILVERS. (*Goes to inspect Billy's hair.*) Look at this, will you. A man works hard for his money, goes to get a decent haircut and look, we got a fungus among us.

CHAVEZ. Let it grow out for a few weeks and stop by the house. Lupe will even it out on the sides.

BILLY. Yea, right, Mr. Chavez, I'd appreciate that.

CHAVEZ. How's your mama and papa?

BILLY. Good. Dad spends a lot of time up at Theodore Wirth Golf Course. During the winter, he's been doing some painting.

SILVERS. I thought he was retired. What's he doing painting?

BILLY. Not house painting, oil painting. He's become an artist. Said he always wanted to be an artist since he was a kid.

SILVERS. That's terrific. I love that, someone following their dreams. Doing things that they always wanted to do but never had time to do.

CHAVEZ. I always wanted to be an actor.

JAMAR. Well, do it, Mr. Chavez!

CHAVEZ. No, shit I'm too old.

BILLY. You're never too old, Mr. Chavez. You remember Ray Wells?

SILVERS. He taught boxing at the old Phyllis Wheatley House?

BILLY. Exactly. Well, he took some beginning acting classes at North Commons. Just did his first play.

CHAVEZ. No kidding. Maybe I should give him a call tomorrow.

SILVERS. Manana, you always say manana.

CHAVEZ. What about you, hombre? All you do in your spare time is sit in front of the T.V. and watch wrestling, that phony crap.

SILVERS. Oh! So now it's phony. Who got me started watching wrestling? You got me started, remember?

CHAVEZ. That was before, when Verne Gagne was champion, and Butch Levy. It's phony now.

SILVERS. Phony schmoney! Verne Gagne couldn't hold Hulk Hogan's shorts. He's a woos!

(The old MEN argue about who's a woos. The KIDS love it.)

JAMAR. Hey! Hey! Hey! Time out! *(Beat.)* How about you, Mr. Silvers? You must have some unfulfilled dreams.

SILVERS. My dream? Well, Milley and I always wanted to go to Israel. After the war, some of our family, the ones that were still alive, left Poland and moved to Israel. It would be nice to go there and meet them.

CHAVEZ. You never told me that.

SILVERS. You never told me you wanted to be another Jeff Chandler.

JAMAR. And Billy here wants to be a hip hop star, right?

BILLY. Right! And when I hit it big, I'm going to bankroll a business for you. Deal homie?

(THEY give each other five.)

JAMAR. Deal homes. What?

BILLY. The van, man.

JAMAR. All right, but I want it back here on Monday morning and gassed up!

BILLY. Alright!

(JAMAR tosses his keys to BILLY who heads for the door.)

JAMAR. And make sure it's defunked when I get it back!

SILVERS. Say hi to your parents for me.

CHAVEZ. Yea, me too. By the way, who did you say cut your hair?

BILLY. Got it cut up at Young Brothers on Plymouth, why?

CHAVEZ. 'Cuz, I'm going to send Lupe up there and show them how to cut hair.

BILLY. Ah ... my dad already talked to them. Thanks, Jamar. Catch ya later. *(BILLY exits.)*

SILVERS. What a nice young man.

CHAVEZ. He sure is, the whole family.

JAMAR. So, Mr. Silvers, any special instructions?

SILVERS. What for?

JAMAR. Because you're going to be gone.

SILVERS. *(This is not easy for Silvers.)* No, no special instructions. Just do what you always do. Don't worry about ordering. I'll do that Monday before I go into the hospital. Most important, make sure you ...

BOTH. Don't keep too much money in the register.

SILVERS. Oh! And make sure you make ...

BOTH. Nightly deposits.

SILVERS. And let's see, what else?

JAMAR. The change order. What about the bills?

SILVERS. Chavez can run them over to Milley and she can do them. Other than that, you know all the rest. I don't expect you to work all the hours so just use your best judgment and close whenever you have to. Any questions? No? Good.

JAMAR. Do you mind if I pick up some things at the hardware store?

SILVERS. Like what?

JAMAR. Oh, just some nuts and bolts. Thought I'd try and fix up some of the display racks.

SILVERS. Well, you can try but those racks have about had it. There's tools and a bunch of hardware down in the old butcher room inside the old Coke machine.

(Enter KAUFMAN and LEWIS.)

LEWIS. Speaking of old machines, Mr. Silvers, you're going to have to clean out that basement. It's really bad down there. It doesn't look like you've ever thrown out anything in the past fifty years.

SILVERS. But some of that stuff is valuable.

KAUFMAN. Well, then sell it. You can use the money to pay for some of the repairs to this dump.

LEWIS. Use a little sugar, Lenora. It's not that damn important. Mr. Silvers, the basement is going to have to be cleaned up.

JAMAR. When Billy brings my van back on Monday, I'll have him give me a hand with some of that stuff. I'm sure Billy won't mind. Is Monday O.K., Mr. Lewis?

CHAVEZ. Your grandpa and I will help.

KAUFMAN. Why not start today? Why put it off? You're in violation, right, Earl? They're in violation.

LEWIS. Monday will be fine.

KAUFMAN. Monday will be fine.

JAMAR. We'll put the good stuff in my mom's garage until you can sell it and the rest of the junk we'll take to the scrap metal yard and see what we can get. (*Pause.*) If that's okay, Mr. Silvers?

SILVERS. Good, good. That' s exactly what I would do.

KAUFMAN. I don't know about that. Moving junk from one place to make a fire hazard in another? We'll have to check with the fire inspector. Where did you say your mother's garage is?

LEWIS. Storing the stuff in your mother's garage will be fine, son.

KAUFMAN. Yes, for a while would be fine ... son.

LEWIS. Now, Mr. Silvers, about these other problems.

KAUFMAN. (*KAUFMAN is delighted that they are now getting to the good stuff.*) I have all the reports here, Earl. Right here. (*SHE starts leafing through them on her clip board.*)

KAUFMAN. Here is my report filed six months ago noting the problems with the wiring and my reports from the last two months and this! Ah! This! The final inspection. It's all in my report. You'll notice I gave him thirty days to have it fixed. Look at the date, Earl, look at the date. (*Looks at watch.*) And we have what? We are now exactly twenty-eight days later. Oh! Don't look at me like I didn't warn you. I warned them, Earl. I warned them. They didn't know who they were messing with.

LEWIS. All right, Lenora. Now they know. Now, Mr. Silvers, the prob ...

KAUFMAN. I warned you.

LEWIS. Lenora, for Christ sake, will you please let me talk!

KAUFMAN. Absolutely, Earl! Absolutely!

LEWIS. (*Sarcastically.*) Thank you. Mr. Silvers, the main problem is this wiring. You were given thirty days to redo the work. Who did the work anyway?

(There is a guilty pause.)

JAMAR. I did most of it. My uncle's an electrician. He helped me with some of it but I did most of the work.

LEWIS. I see ... well, the fact remains that some of the work doesn't meet code and a work permit wasn't pulled. More importantly, you were given thirty days notice, Mr. Silvers.

SILVERS. Some of the work? But Mrs. Kaufman made it sound like all the wiring had to be redone and the bids I got ... (*HE gets bids from under the counter.*) Look at these! The cheapest is over four thousand dollars. That's money I don't have. I mean, look around you. Does it look like I can afford that kind of money?

LEWIS. Then you should have called downtown and talked to someone.

SILVERS. Call who? Mrs. Kaufman here didn't seem to want to reason with me. She just told me what was going to happen if I didn't get the work done. It frightened me.

LEWIS. Not everyone that works downtown is unreasonable, Mr. Silvers, and if you expect justice, you have to learn that yes, you can fight City Hall. Frankly, I don't see as many problems as Mrs. Kaufman does. What did you say your name is, son?

JAMAR. Jamar Mooney.

LEWIS. Jamar here did a pretty good job overall. Mooney? Say, you're not related to Elvis Mooney, are you?

JAMAR. He's my grandfather.

LEWIS. Well, I'll be damned. It's a small world. Your grandpa coached me in little league baseball over at the Emmanuel Cohen Center.

CHAVEZ. Butchie Lewis!! Goddamn it the hell! Remember me? Joe Chavez!

LEWIS. Joe Chavez! Carlos Chavez' dad?

CHAVEZ. Yes sir!!!!

LEWIS. Well, I'll be ... hey, Jamar. Joe's son, Carlos, was the best damn third baseman that ever came out of North Minneapolis. Played with him in little league, then at North High. (*Beat.*) Carlos' death was a big loss for all of us, Mr. Chavez.

CHAVEZ. Thanks. I'll tell Carlos' mother you remembered. She'll like that.

(*THEY shake hands.*)

KAUFMAN. That's fine, fine, and very heartwarming, but what about this thirty-day notice, Earl?

LEWIS. Oh! Stuff a sock in it, Lenora. Well, this seems like a reunion of the old Northside.

SILVERS. You played for the Emmanuel Cohen Center? Lewis? Lewis? Don't tell me? You're a Northside Jewboy?

LEWIS. Absolutely!

(SILVERS goes to Lewis and slaps him on the back.)

SILVERS. Finally!!! Someone I can do business with.

LEWIS. Okay! Then, let's get down to business. First of all, I'm going to give you another two weeks to begin the work.

KAUFMAN. What!! You can't do that! You're showing favoritism, Lewis!!

LEWIS. Lenora, why don't you wait in the car.

KAUFMAN. I'll be waiting in the car. *(KAUFMAN crosses to the door.)*

KAUFMAN and LEWIS. *(Under their breath.)* Asshole!

LEWIS. Well, Mr. Silvers, here's the story. You get Jamar's uncle, the electrician, over here to look at this report, have him draw up some plans and bring them down to my office. I'll look them over and make any corrections. Then, we'll jerk a permit for the work. Jamar can do most of the work and his uncle can do the rest. It'll save you a ton of money. Now, I can only extend this for two weeks. You understand?

SILVERS. I understand. But what about the rest of the violations? The plumbing, heating and the rest?

LEWIS. We'll worry about them later. I can stall them. Right now, our main concern is Lenora. Let's get her out of your hair first. Okay?

SILVERS. Okay.
CHAVEZ. This sure is a big load off our mind, amigo.

(LEWIS starts for door.)

SILVERS. (*Moved.*) I don't know what to say. I don't know how to thank you.
LEWIS. My pleasure. I consider it an honor to help a legend.
SILVERS. A legend?
LEWIS. Yea, the king of the kosher grocers, every Northsider knows that. Shalom.
SILVERS. Shalom.

(LEWIS exits.)

SILVERS. Jamar, let's get to work.

(LIGHTS fade to BLACK as ACT II ends.)

ACT III

As LIGHTS come up we see a completely transformed Silvers' Market. All the display shelves are fixed and completely stocked. There are new curtains in the windows. The store is spotless. Along one wall we see one video display with signs advertising the rentals and movie posters. The deli case is full. The phone is now cordless. Hanging plants decorate the store and a ceiling fan slowly turns above. We hear soft MUZAK. The bell over the door is replaced with a soft chime. We see JAMAR dusting and straightening shelves. HE is still immaculate. BILLY, who is also in sharp uniform, is carrying out boxes to van and passes MOONEY as HE goes out door.

BILLY. Morning, Mr. Mooney.
MOONEY. Morning, Billy.

(MOONEY checks out sidewalk, then the bag of rock salt which is in its proper place. HE opens and shuts door to hear the new CHIME. HE doesn't like it. BILLY reenters. MOONEY is obviously in the way.)
BILLY. Excuse me, Mr. Mooney.

(Squeezing past Mooney HE goes quickly to basement. After beat, SILVERS comes in squeezing past Mooney like a revolving door. SILVERS is carrying the same

*box BILLY has just thrown out. HE is obviously very
tired and has developed a cough.)*

SILVERS. I haven't looked through all of these boxes
yet!
MOONEY. Chimes?
SILVERS. What?!!
MOONEY. Chimes. Your idea?

*(SILVERS is irritated. Says nothing but points to Jamar.
It's his idea, not mine.)*

MOONEY. Milley called yet ...?
SILVERS. Don't even ask! No one counts anymore.
These kids nowadays have no respect for tradition, I don't
understand it.
MOONEY. I heard that.
JAMAR. Here, Mr. Silvers, let me get that for you.
SILVERS. I've got it, I've got it, no problem.
BILLY. Coffee?

*(MOONEY confused, nods yes and BILLY hands him
coffee cup on saucer and a cocktail napkin. BILLY is
very formal. MOONEY tastes and something is wrong.)*

BILLY. French roast. You like?

*(SILVERS is very disgusted, MOONEY gestures to
Silvers "Whose?" and SILVERS again throws a point
to Jamar.)*

BILLY. Cookie? (*Holding plate.*)

(BOTH MEN do double take. This really disgusts SILVERS as BILLY goes to van. MOONEY goes to sit down and finds cushion on his chair. HE throws it on the floor.)

MOONEY. This place is getting too damn comfortable. *(About cookie.)* Not bad. Where's Chavez?

JAMAR. Shit!! Forgot. He called and asked if you could run him over to the post office to pick up a registered letter.

MOONEY. What's wrong with his car?

JAMAR. I don't know. That's what he said. Maybe Lupe's got it. He wanted you to pick him up first thing.

MOONEY. Guess I'll finish my French roast and get on over there then. *(Sips.)* Hmmmm.

SILVERS. What are you doing over there?

JAMAR. Just moving some stock around.

SILVERS. What stock? Don't move the stock around unless I tell you to. It confuses me when I'm looking for things.

JAMAR. Well, I just thought the bags of snacks would sell better over here.

SILVERS. No, no, no. Those are impulse buys. They sell better closer to the register. Believe me, I know.

JAMAR. But Mr. Silvers, I just thought that when people come by this area since the pop coolers are over here, they would see the chips and stuff and would be more likely to pick up a bag. I know I would.

SILVERS. *(Thinks about what Jamar has just said.)* You would?

JAMAR. Yea.

SILVERS. Huh. Okay, so put the chips over there. We ll try it out for awhile. (*Stops and thinks about Jamar's idea for awhile.*) Huh. (*Looks at Mooney.*) I knew that.

MOONEY. Don't have to tell me. (*Gets up.*) Feel like I should leave a tip. You got anything you want me to do on the way?

SILVERS. Well ...

JAMAR. (*Without looking up.*) No Grandpa, got everything under control ... totally.

(*SILVERS burns.*)

MOONEY. Well, I'll see ya later. See ya, Jamar.
JAMAR. See ya, Gramps.

(*As MOONEY leaves the PHONE rings.*)

JAMAR. Tell Milley I said hi.
SILVERS. What! Hello, sweetheart ... I'm fine, thank you ... what? ... French roast? ... Yes, I'll bring you home a cup ... Yes, and a cookie ... No, I haven't tried them yet ... I love you, too. Bye, sweetheart. (*HE coughs.*) Gaddamn cough, always get one come springtime.

JAMAR. You okay, Mr. Silvers?

SILVERS. Fine, fine. Just a little tired. Whew!! I got to get off of my feet for a moment.

(*SILVERS sits as EARL LEWIS enters.*)

LEWIS. Hi, Mr. Silvers. Hi, Jamar.
JAMAR. Hi, Mr. Lewis.

LEWIS. Was just in the neighborhood and thought I'd stop by and see how the rest of the work has been going.

SILVERS. Fine, just fine.

JAMAR. My friend, Billy, is just taking out the last of the junk from the basement.

SILVERS. It's not all junk.

JAMAR. There's just a few boxes of old papers down in Mr. Silvers' office.

(BILLY comes up.)

SILVERS. Well, don't throw any papers out until I look through them.

LEWIS. I take it this is Billy.

BILLY. You got it. *(Puts down box.)* Would you like...

SILVERS. *(Jumps in with big smile.)* Coffee?

LEWIS. No.

SILVERS. Cookie?

LEWIS. No thanks. I'm an inspector, not a policeman. Say, business must be getting pretty good with you putting someone else on the payroll.

BILLY. Just passing time.

SILVERS. He's working for tips.

LEWIS. Oh! I like the new metal ceiling. Bet that cost you a pretty penny.

SILVERS. What ceiling? *(Sees LEWIS looking up, puts on glasses, sees new ceiling and gives Jamar a quick glare.)* Oh, this ceiling!! I thought you were talking ... yes, well actually it's the old ceiling. I covered it up many years ago when acoustical tile was in fashion.

LEWIS. So whose idea?

JAMAR. Well, Billy and I ...

SILVERS. Mine! ... I have been thinking about doing it for years.

(JAMAR is bothered.)

LEWIS. Your ideas and the young men's muscle, good combination.

SILVERS. Yes, the Hills Brothers.

LEWIS. The what?

SILVERS. Nothing.

LEWIS. I drove by the other night and saw Jamar and Billy working on the ceiling, and wondered, what in the heck is Jamar working on now? Hell, it was after midnight. Hope you're not paying overtime. (*HE laughs but Silvers doesn't know about it.*)

SILVERS. Well, we do what we have to do, right Jamar?

(JAMAR doesn't answer.)

LEWIS. Say, how you been feeling, Mr. Silvers?

SILVERS. Fine. Doctor wants me to take it easy for a few more weeks, then he said we'll take another look.

LEWIS. Well, you're damn lucky ...

SILVERS. A close call.

LEWIS. ... to have a guy like Jamar to look after things for you. Yes, sir, he's a real find.

SILVERS. A real find, yes.

LEWIS. He sure won over the Inspections Department.

SILVERS. Is that so?

LEWIS. Got all the work done, and the inspectors say he did a better job than most professional contractors.

SILVERS. That's nice.

LEWIS. Yea, he's a real talented young man. I understand business is really picking up, too. This kid's breathing new life into your old business.

SILVERS. (*Stung.*) There are no new ideas, Mr. Lewis, just old ones that haven't been done yet.

LEWIS. (*Realizing he has struck a nerve.*) Right, right. Well, I'd better shove off. Oh! By the way, here's a copy of the city ordinance on sidewalk cafes I promised Jamar I'd drop off.

SILVERS. (*Doesn't know what he is talking about.*) Sidewalk cafe? ... Oh, yes! ... sidewalk cafes.

LEWIS. I talked to the sidewalk inspector and he says he doesn't see a problem with you putting some tables out front. Of course, you'll have to get approval from your alderman.

JAMAR. He already said it's okay, he ... stopped ... by ... for ... coffee.

LEWIS. How many tables you going to put out there?

SILVERS. Oh? (*Looks to JAMAR who holds up six fingers.*) Six!!

LEWIS. You going to get a license to let people drink beer out there on those hot summer nights?

SILVERS. Of course!! ... (*But JAMAR is shaking his head no.*) Not. Of course not!!

(This game humors JAMAR who just smiles. This bothers SILVERS)

LEWIS. I'll bet that's ... (*LEWIS joins the game and plays eenee meene with the two.*) ... your idea?

SILVERS. Yes.

(JAMAR gives Silvers a dirty look)

LEWIS. Well, I think it's one hell of an idea. Good for you. Well, you two take care.

SILVERS. See you, Mr. Lewis.

JAMAR. See ya, Earl.

LEWIS. See ya, Jamar.

(As LEWIS leaves, SILVERS gives JAMAR a glare that could cut through glass.)

SILVERS. See ya, Earl? Earl!!!

JAMAR. I know you're angry with me, Mr. Silvers. But I just thought it was a good idea and I just wanted to get some information about it before I brought it up to you.

SILVERS. Just like you tore down the ceiling tile and cleaned up the metal ceiling to surprise me, just like you started making sandwiches and pizza by the slice, and the videos and the expensive mineral waters.

JAMAR. But it's paying for itself and business is starting to boom. Mr. Silvers, have you ever thought of ...

SILVERS. Wait! Let's just stop for a second. Let's just hold on just one second here. I can't do this, I can't work like this anymore. This is my business and it's out of control!

JAMAR. I know it's your business, Mr. Silvers.

SILVERS. That's right and that means there is only one boss and I am the only one who can make these decisions. *(Pause.)* No more! No more new stuff, no more ideas!!

(PHONE rings.)

JAMAR. Mrs. Cohen.
SILVERS. Mrs. Feinstein.
JAMAR. Mrs. Cohen.
SILVERS. Mrs. Feinstein.

(THEY race to the phone. JAMAR wins.)

JAMAR. Good morning, Silvers' Market ... *(Gives thumbs up.)* Good morning, Mrs. Cohen, how are you today?
SILVERS. Well, I was close. They're related. Bet you didn't know that ... Mr. Coffee.
JAMAR. ... Yup ... yup ... right. The tortillas are fresh this morning ... okay, I'll send over a dozen ... some milk ... one loaf of bread ... got some fresh cracked wheat ... great! One loaf of cracked wheat.
SILVERS. Tell her I said hello.
JAMAR. *(Not hearing.)* Oh! By the way, I had Mrs. Chavez make up some recipe cards and I made some copies for you, you know because I know how much you like her tortillas.

(SILVERS watches Jamar, impressed but a little jealous.)

SILVERS. Tell her I said hi.
JAMAR. *(Acknowledges Silvers.)* Mr. Silvers says hi ... what? ... well, the recipe cards show you how you can do different things with tortillas like quesadillas. Quesadillas ... they're like cheese sandwiches made with a

tortilla and jack cheese, they're real easy to eat with the trouble I know you have with your teeth.

SILVERS. Great! Now he's a dentist.

JAMAR. Monterey Jack ... right ... *(To Silvers.)* Can I send her over a sample?

SILVERS. Sure, why not?

JAMAR. I'm going to send you over a little sample ... great, anything else? ... Okay, I'll run it right over, Mrs. Cohen. Thanks so much for the order. Bye now.

(JAMAR takes out bag and quickly packs up Mrs. Cohen's order as SILVERS watches.)

SILVERS. Bye now? Why do you say "Bye now?"

JAMAR. Huh?

SILVERS. You just said "Bye now." Why don't you just say "Bye"?

JAMAR. *(Not really paying attention.)* Just a figure of speech. I'm going to run this over to Mrs. Cohen's real quick, you gonna be okay?

SILVERS. Of course, I'm going to be okay But Chavez delivers to Mrs. Cohen.

JAMAR. She wants it right away so I told her that I would bring it right over. But if you need me here, I guess she could wait for awhile.

SILVERS. No. Go, go ahead.

JAMAR. *(Dashes for door.)* I'll be back in a flash. Billy's downstairs if you need anything.

SILVERS. So what's he doing down there, Mr. Keebler, baking cookies?

JAMAR. No, he has a secret source. Aren't they great?

SILVERS. I haven't tasted them. *(Sarcastically.)* "Bye now."

(JAMAR runs out as PHONE rings, SILVERS slowly gets up to answer. As HE gets to the phone after many rings, it stops ringing.)

SILVERS. Hello? Hello? Must have been in a hurry. Everyone's in a hurry.

(SILVERS hangs up phone, starts to walk back to chair and stops and leans against counter, HE's having another chest pain. As pain fades, HE gathers himself, and reflects on the store and all the changes that are occurring and goes to chair. As HE sits, the PHONE begins to ring again, but this time HE just watches as the PHONE rings five or six times and then stops. BILLY comes up with box. HE looks at phone, then at SILVERS with concern.)

SILVERS. Wrong number.

(BILLY pauses. Then picks up cordless phone and gives it to Silvers and exits. SILVERS dials home.)

SILVERS. Hello, sweetheart? ... Yes, it's me! Who else calls you, sweetheart? ... Did you just call? ... Oh, no I just thought it sounded like your ring ... Yes, I'm glad I called too ... how are you feeling? ... Well, I'm ... I'm feeling a little tired today ... No ... No, I'm not going to stay too long today, just a few hours and then I'll be home ... I have to stay a few hours dear ... well, it's been busy down here ... I know Jamar can handle it but it's still my store and I have things to do ... Well, the problem is is that you're getting too used to me being at home, you're going to have to get over that ... Why? ... Why do you think? ... When I'm feeling better, I can put in more hours and start cutting back on Jamar's hours, that's why. He doesn't work for free ... please don't argue with me, sweetheart, I promise I'll just be down here for a few hours ... No, I won't lift anything heavy ... cross my heart, hope to ... well, I'll just cross my heart if that's okay? ... Okay, bye, Oh! And one more thing sweetheart, do you, do you know what a quesadilla is? ... Never mind, I love you too. Bye.

(SILVERS hangs up as BILLY enters.)

BILLY. Hey, where'd Jamar go to?

SILVERS. He went on a delivery and I'm fine, thank you!!

BILLY. What's wrong?

SILVERS. I don't know, Billy, I don't know what's going on with me. I think I'm just ...

BILLY. (*Starts for basement.*) Got the blues, Mr. Silvers, you got the blues. I'm gonna take those last few boxes out of the basement. (*As HE starts for the basement, HE grabs a soda out of the deli case and starts for the stairs.*)

SILVERS. What are you doing?

BILLY. Just getting the last of the box ...

SILVERS. No, no. (*Points to the soda.*)

BILLY. What this? Jamar said it was okay.

SILVERS. (*Sarcastically.*) Oh! Well! If Jamar says it's okay!!!

(*BILLY goes downstairs as PHONE rings.*)

SILVERS. Good morning, Silvers' Market ... No, Jamar's not here. This is Mr. Silvers, the owner of the market speaking ... what! Do we have Halloween, too? Of course, we have Halloween too, schmuck!! The Jews celebrate all the holidays!!! (*HE slams phone down.*) Goddamn crank calls ... Do we have Halloween, too.

(*JAMAR returns a little out of breath.*)

SILVERS. What? You forget something? See, that's what happens when you're in such a hurry.

JAMAR. No, I didn't forget anything, Mr. Silvers. I'm back.

SILVERS. Well, I know you're back but why so soon?

JAMAR. It's only three blocks away. Is Billy done yet?

SILVERS. No. He's in the basement drinking free soda! You should have been back sooner so you could have talked to one of your wise guy friends. He asked me if we have Halloween, too.

JAMAR. (*As HE's going to video rack.*) Well, we have it, don't we?

SILVERS. (*Not looking at Jamar.*) Of course we do!

JAMAR. Yea, here it is. How come you didn't rent it?

SILVERS. (*Realizing mistake.*) Well ... because Milley wanted me to bring it home to watch it this evening.

JAMAR. Are you sure she wants to see this?

SILVERS. Of course I'm sure, why would I make it up?

JAMAR. It's just that it's so full of blood and gore.

SILVERS. We like blood and gore, the gorier the better.

JAMAR. Okay, but don't say I didn't warn you!

(Enter BILLY carrying a box of old papers.)

BILLY. You wanna look through this, Mr. Silvers?

SILVERS. *(To Billy.)* Wait. *(To Jamar.)* What? What did you just say? You warn me!! Listen here, you watch how you talk to me, young man. I've been here fifty years and I don't need some young kid to warn me! Goddamn it.

JAMAR. *(Confused and embarrassed.)* I didn't mean ...

SILVERS. I know what you meant! You think because I'm an old man that I can't fend for myself, just because I'm a little under the weather. I've been worse. Did you know I got shot once! Yes, I got shot! Two young punks came in that door, one grabbed me around the neck and the other one went for the cash. I kicked the one in the nuts and the other one shot me in the side. But they didn't get the money and the store was only closed for two days!! Two days!! So you don't warn me!!!

(JAMAR and BILLY are confused and there is an uneasy silence.)

JAMAR. I'm sorry, Mr. Silvers ... I ... I ...

SILVERS. No, no don't apologize ... It's not you ... It's me. I should apologize. I'm sorry. I don't know what's going on with me lately ... It's just ... It's just ... It's just those gaddamn cookies!! Whose idea was that anyway?

(The PHONE rings. THEY all look, THEY all smile, THEY all laugh.)

SILVERS. Hello sweetheart ... yes, I just found out ... I think it was a wonderful idea ... of course, I tasted them, they were delicious, they're a smash hit ... yes, sweetheart, I love you, too. Bye. *(In mock rage, shaking fists and moving toward them.)* Why you little shits! Trying to pull a fast one over on the old Jew. Why I oughta ...

(JAMAR and BILLY back up in mock terror.)

JAMAR. No, please, Mr. Silvers. Remember your heart.

BILLY. My god! Someone stop him, he's going to reopen that gunshot wound!!

(Enter CHAVEZ and MOONEY. THEY are very excited. MOONEY is waiving registered letter he just picked up at post office. THEY come in door dancing and hollering.)

SILVERS. What? What's going on? What?

CHAVEZ. The letter! The registered letter!!! Ha, ha ahhhhh!

SILVERS. Let me see. *(HE grabs letter and begins to read but has misplaced his glasses.)*

MOONEY. This calls for a celebration! I'm buyin'. (*MOONEY goes to beer cooler and gets out a six-pack and opens cans.*)

BILLY. What's going on, Jamar?

JAMAR. Hell if I know.

SILVERS. I haven't got my glasses, Jamar! Read this, will you?

(*JAMAR takes letter and quickly scans it and begins to holler and jump up and down joining MOONEY and CHAVEZ. BILLY reads.*)

BILLY. Holy shit!!!

SILVERS. Will someone tell me what's going on?

JAMAR. We're rich, Mr. Silvers!! We're rich!! Aaaahhhhh!!!!!

SILVERS. Goddamn it, stop!!!!

(*THEY all simmer down.*)

CHAVEZ. We're rich, Silvers!

SILVERS. What do you mean, we're rich? Now simmer down and just tell me what the hell you're talking about.

CHAVEZ. I got a call from my grandson, Kenny, this morning. He works at the post office, right? Well, he said, Grandpa, there's a registered letter down here for you from a lawyer in Chicago. And then he said that Mooney had one down there, too ... Jesus Christ, we're rich!!!

SILVERS. Mooney! For Christ sakes, what? What?!

MOONEY. So I pick up Chavez and we go down to Loring Station. We get down there and I open my letter and it says that Mrs. Goldstein's estate has been settled and she left me fifteen thousand dollars. That wonderful, beautiful woman left me fifteen thousand dollars!

CHAVEZ. And she left me five thousand dollars, Izzie! Can you believe it!

SILVERS. Unbelievable!

MOONEY. She said she wanted ten thousand to go to me and five thousand to go to Jamar for his education.

JAMAR. What!! *(Grabs letter.)* Where does it say that? I didn't see that!

MOONEY. Right there, son.

JAMAR. *(Stunned.)* But I didn't hardly even know the woman. Why Gramps?

MOONEY. Oh, I managed to brag about you here and there.

BILLY. Hey man, don't look a gift horse in the mouth.

MOONEY. I told you not to let go of your dreams, boy. Dreams are awful powerful. We all admire people that have them and she wanted to be part of your dream, son.

BILLY. I don't know if we feel very comfortable around all these wealthy men. Right, Mr. Silvers?

(THEY all realize that SILVERS has been left out and there is an uneasy moment.)

SILVERS. But look at all the business Mrs. Goldstein gave me all of these years.

CHAVEZ. *(Pause.)* Yes, that's true.

MOONEY. Ah, right, right.

SILVERS. I'm happy for you, son. You deserve it, gaddamn it, you all deserve it. So what are you going to do with all that money?

CHAVEZ. Well, first, I'm going to take those acting lessons, then I'm going to take Lupe on a trip to Mexico to visit family.

MOONEY. I'm putting this money in the bank and just sit on it for awhile. I think it's best if I just sit on it for awhile out of respect for Mrs. Goldstein.

SILVERS. And Jamar, now you've got enough money to take care of your education, I suppose you'll want to get enrolled as soon as possible?

JAMAR. Yea.

MOONEY. You could probably go to the U with that kind of money.

JAMAR. Well, it's a start ... but ah ... there's still a lot to do around here and when Mr. Silvers gets on his feet, then maybe I'll look into taking some classes again.

SILVERS. Nonsense! Your education is more important. This place can take care of itself. I'll be here another fifty years. Get your degree, get rich and spend a lot of money here.

CHAVEZ. You don't sound too excited about it.

JAMAR. I know everyone wants what's best for me. Gramps, you do and Mr. Silvers and Mr. Chavez and everybody, even Mrs. Goldstein, but my dreams don't include school right now. I just want to work here and learn more. You see, Gramps, I like it here. I like what I'm doing. I know Mr. Silvers can't afford to pay me much but that's okay. This is what I want to do, at least until Mr. Silvers comes back to work full time.

SILVERS. You know, Jamar, I told you as soon as I get better I'm going to have to cut your hours and that hasn't changed. Besides, it would be a shame to let that money go to waste if you don't go to school.

MOONEY. No. That's out of the question. That money was left for your education.

JAMAR. Okay, then I'll give the money to Mr. Silvers.

SILVERS. What? Why give me the money?

JAMAR. Because this is my school. I've learned more from you than any school teacher ever taught me. You never make me feel stupid. I watch you, Mr. Silvers. I've watched you ever since Grandpa brought me in here when I was a little boy.

SILVERS. But why, son? Why would you want to waste your life like me? I'm a nobody.

JAMAR. Nobody except your own man. I mean, look at this place. This is you. You built it up and took care of it and took care of the people who live around here. I've seen your books. I know some of these people around here get special prices. Everyone respects you and someday I want some of that same respect.

SILVERS. Achh! It's just good business.

BILLY. It's more than just that, Mr. Silvers. I know what Jamar's talking about. It's been like that for a lot of the kids around here.

SILVERS. Ach! No loitering is not Yiddish for I love you. (*PHONE rings. SILVERS answers.*) I can't talk now sweetheart. I'm getting stroked. (*Hangs up.*) So what else?

(*THEY all enjoy the moment.*)

CHAVEZ. We love you, cabron. Look at you, amigo, "El rey de los mercados, kosher."

SILVERS. Wha ...?

CHAVEZ. The king of the kosher grocers.

MOONEY. You'll always be king.

SILVERS. Well ... Jamar, you can't give me the money because that would make you my partner. That I don't need. I'm too young to retire, I'll never retire but I' ll tell you what ... you can continue to work here part-time and continue to learn, but no new ideas.

JAMAR. Okay.

CHAVEZ. I know. How about I take everyone to White Castle for sliders to celebrate?

MOONEY. I'm up for that. Now that you can afford it. What about the deliveries?

BILLY. I'll be here all day, promised Jamar I'd do some painting.

SILVERS. Painting? What painting?

BILLY. The front of the store.

(JAMAR smiles guiltily. There is another tense moment.)

SILVERS. That's a good idea.

CHAVEZ. What about you, Izzie? You gonna join us?

SILVERS. No. Doctor says I got to watch my diet.

MOONEY. Come on, Izzie, it won't be no fun without you.

BILLY. Go on, Mr. Silvers. You don't have to eat nothin', you can look at all the honeys. That'll get the old heart pumpin'.

JAMAR. Yea, go on, Mr. Silvers. It'll be good for you.

SILVERS. Okay, okay. I'll meet you fellas up there in a while. I just want to go through this box of old papers so Billy can get rid of the rest.

CHAVEZ. Okay, but don't be too long. Open the goddamn door, I'm rich now!!!!

(CHAVEZ and MOONEY exit.)

SILVERS. You know, fellas, when I see those two like that, it takes me back fifty years when I first met the two of them.

BILLY. Damn, you known them that long, Mr. Silvers?

SILVERS. Well, sure. Now, let's see what we have in the is old box ... ach! Just old junk, old mementos that I don't even remember what I saved them for.

JAMAR. *(Takes out old picture.)* Hey man, look at this! An old picture of the store.

BILLY. Damn! The store looked all new 'n shit.

SILVERS. *(Looks at picture.)* Yes, this gentlemen, is what the store looked like in the golden days of the old Northside.

JAMAR. There's tables in front!

SILVERS. Yup! Six of them.

(JAMAR enjoys the moment. He's been had.)

BILLY. Who's this geek lookin' motherfucker?

SILVERS. That geek looking motherfucker ... would be me.

BILLY. Sorry I dogged you, Mr. Silvers.

SILVERS. Oh, that's okay. With a haircut like yours, I just consider the source. Now go get the other boxes, Mr. Geek Buster.

BILLY. Mr. Silvers, you're dopest, deafest, most chillinest, G-man, you know what I'm sayin'?

SILVERS. Does that mean like groovy?

BILLY. (*Beat.*) No. (*Leaves.*)

JAMAR. Who's this old man?

SILVERS. Oh! That's old, Mr. Johanssen. This picture was taken when I was still working for him here. I worked for him for three years. The poor old man, he couldn't quit, wouldn't quit. This store was his whole reason for existence. And even when I started doing most of the work and started to build the business, he just couldn't see the handwriting on the wall ... (*Hears himself.*) I remember him telling me once that the worst part about being your own boss was that there was no one to tell you when to quit ... then one day he died. (*Points to door.*) Fell down right out there. (*Pause.*) And then it was my turn and I became the king of the kosher grocers. (*HE sadly sees the truth.*)

JAMAR. Well, let me go get your coat for you, Mr. Silvers.

SILVERS. No. Wait. We have to talk. Sit.

(*SILVERS rises and offers JAMAR his chair and JAMAR sits. SILVERS surveys his store, his life. HE is about to do the hardest thing he has ever done in his life.*)

SILVERS. I told you son that I wouldn't take your money because I don't need a partner, right?

JAMAR. Yes.

SILVERS. Well, I tell you what I will do. After you discuss this with your mother and your grandfather ...

(*Pause.*) I will take that money as a down payment on this store.

JAMAR. (*Stunned.*) I'll talk it over with them.

SILVERS. Good.

JAMAR. Mr. Silvers. I'll take good care of this store.

SILVERS. Jamar, Jamar, you already have. (*THEY shake.*) And now, there's one more thing I have to tell you and this is very, very important. Don't forget the faces of the people who come through that door. Because one day, they're going to be old and they're going to look to you for help.

(*The PHONE rings.*)

SILVERS. Yes sweetheart ... yes ... a what? A registered letter? ... from Chicago ... I'll be home in an hour. Pack your bags, sweetheart ... why? ... We're going to Israel.

(*MUSIC up. Fade to BLACK.*)

END OF PLAY

COSTUME PLOT

IZZY SILVERS
<u>Act I</u>
Black 1950's pleated pants
White cotton shirt
Grey sweater w/shawl collar
Black clip-on tie
Black & grey suspenders
High-top formal shoes
Half glasses on string around neck
Black overcoat
Grey medium brim Fedora w/black band
Black socks
Grey scarf
Black gloves
Wedding band
ADD: Dirty white apron w/bib
<u>Act II</u>
Same as Act I:
    Hat
    Overcoat, scarf, gloves
    Shoes, socks
    Shirt
    Glasses
    Wedding band
Navy blue 1950's style suit
Black vinyl briefcase
Blue clip-on bow tie
Navy blue suspenders
Clean white bib apron

Act III
    Same as Act I:
    Overcoat, hat
    Shirt, sweater
    Black socks
    Wedding band
    (no scarf, no gloves)
Grey 1950's style pleated pants
Black clip-on tie w/stripe
Grey suspenders
Black wing tip shoes
Clean white bib apron

JAMAR MOONEY
Act I
Black sweatshirt
Black sweat pants
White & black Reebok tennis shoes
White socks
Leather Africa medallion
Orange Syracuse starter Jacket
"X" cap
ADD: Dirty white bib apron
Act II
Brown/rust pleated rayon pants
Brown/Rust print rayon shirt
Brown socks
Black belt
Black "Doc Martin" shoes
Act III
White rayon shirt
Black rayon pants

Narrow black tie
Black belt
Black loafers
Syracuse starter jacket
Clean white bib apron

ELVIS MOONEY
<u>Act</u> I
Brown Tweed 1950's style suit w/pleated pants
Tan nylon seersucker shirt
Tan suspenders
Handkerchief
Brown & white two tone shoes
Brown socks
Tank style undershirt
Black & silver glasses
Black cashmere overcoat (somewhat worn)
Tan wide brim Fedora w/brown band
Tan scarf
<u>Act</u> II
Same as Act I (no scarf/gloves)
<u>Act</u> III
Same as Act I (no overcoat)
<u>Change for last scene:</u>
Red Hawaiian shirt
Gold sweater w/suede front
Straw hat

JOE CHAVEZ
<u>Act</u> I
Grey wool old fashioned golf cap w/brim
Grey jacket w/black fake fur collar

Black knitted muffler
Black gloves (worn)
Brown Dicky work pants
Brown plaid acrylic shirt
Regular T-shirt Wide belt w/large buckle
Wire rim glasses w/thick lenses wedding band
Steel toe work shoes (low top)
White socks
Act II
Same as Act I:
    Cap
    Jacket
    Shoes
    Socks
    Belt
    Ring
Blue Dicky work pants
Red plaid flannel shirt
Act III
Same as Act I:
    Shoes
    Socks cap
    Ring
Green Dicky work pants
Wine plaid flannel shirt
Light weight cloth jacket (brown/tan)

LENORA KAUFMAN
Act I
Grey wool pleated slacks
Flat black shoes
Knee high hose

Red sweater
Black & tan jacket w/velvet collar
Black scarf
Black leather gloves
Black leather shoulder bag
Act II
Blue raw silk suit (ill-fitting)
Khaki trench coat
Faux pearls
Low black pumps
Silk scarf
Black leather shoulder bag (As Act I)

BILLY
Act II
Black Nike high tops
White athletic socks
Sunglasses
Raiders starter jacket
Jeans (4 sizes large in waist)
Gold long sleeved T-shirt
Chicago Bulls cap (red)
Black belt
8"-10" diameter clock on string around neck
Act III
Same as Act II:
    Shoes
    Socks
Black tail coat & pants
Wing collar tux shirt
Royal blue bow tie & cummerbund
Top hat

Sunglasses (w/colorful frames)
Pocket watch on chain around neck

EARL LEWIS
<u>Act</u> II
Black trench coat (nice, conservative)
Navy suit (nice, not too trendy)
White button down shirt
Blue & red stripe tie
Black loafers
Black socks
Black belt
<u>Act</u> III
Khaki pants
Brown loafers
Brown socks
Red "Minnesota Twins" polo shirt
Twins cap
Brown belt
"Members Only" jacket, red

PROPERTY PLOT

SET PROPS

Deli Counter
Cooler
Counter w/Cash Register
Small Cabinet w/ coffee pot
3 chairs
Small Table
Grocery shelves, stocked
<u>ACT I—On Stage Preset</u>

By Front Door:
    Bag of sidewalk salt w/cup

Outside of Front Door:

    Bundle of five (5) Newspapers

Deli Counter:

Chalk board
Cup with chalk
Eraser (rag)
Jamar's Off white apron (draped on edge of chalk board)
CD Boom Box (under counter)
Six pack Bud Light (in cooler)

Cash Register Counter:

Clipboard w/store inventory

Cup w/pencils
Carbon order pad
stock of grocery bags (below counter)
Cordless phone (below counter)
SMOKING PERMITTED sign (Magnetic, on cash
    register)
Postcard from Israel (on cash register)

In Drawer:
    SMOKING PROHIBITED sign (magnetic)
    Receipt cards
    Pack of Lucky Strikes with lighter in ashtray
    Silver's Pill Bottle

On Coffee Cabinet:
    1 Pre-measured bag of decaf coffee
    Pitcher water
    4 Styrofoam cups (on narrow tray)
    1 White ceramic mug (on narrow tray)
    Box of sugar cubes (on narrow tray)

In Coffee Cabinet:
    Box sugar cubes
    Identical decanter coffee
    Identical narrow tray:
        White cup & saucer,
        White plate w/4 cookies
        Waiter towel
Small backgammon board
1 "X" Mug with pre measured bag of coffee
1 Spare pre measured bag of coffee

CENTER STAGE ROTATING SHELF UNIT Stock Shelf
  #1:[*]
    3 Boxes corn flakes
    3 Boxes Rice Krispies
    2 Boxes bran & raisin
    4 Ten-lb bags flour

Stock Shelf #2:
    4 Boxes iodized salt
    3 Jars peanut butter
    6 Cans collard greens
    3 Bottles jalapeno peppers
    4 Boxes Malt-o-Meal
    3 Boxes Matzo crackers
    14 Cans chicken noodle soup
    3 Large cans tomato juice

Stock Shelf #3:
    2 Boxes powdered milk
    4 Boxes snack crackers
    12 Boxes macaroni & cheese
    4 Jars pickles
    3 Jars mayonnaise
    3 Jars mustard
    3 Jars ketchup

Stock Shelf # 4
    12 Coffee bricks
    4 Boxes saltine crackers

---

[*] Note: Act I & II grocery shelves are sparsely filled with generic brands. For Act III, items on shelves are name brands and numbers of each item may be increased.

4 Cans powdered chocolate
4 Microwave popcorn
2 Large boxes potato chips

SMALL (SR) ROTATING SHELF UNIT
Stock Shelf #1:
    Shampoo
    Shaving cream
    Tooth paste

Stock Shelf #2:
    Psyllum husk laxative
    Pine cleaner
    Powdered cleanser

Stock Shelf #3:
    4 Large jars of Petroleum Jelly
    4 Large jars of Hair Pomade

Stock Shelf #4:
    4 Packages ant traps
    4 Boxes Brillo pads

OFF STAGE PROP PRESETS (All Off Stage Right)

Snow shovel
Bag of apples
Black satchel containing:
    Money bag w/
        1 roll pennies 1 roll nickles
        1 roll dimes
        banded pack of $1's

Small white pharmacy bag w/bottle pills
2 Bundles newspapers
Pitcher of water
1 paper cup w/water
2 Clip boards w/carbon forms
2 Brown bags each w/ 4 plastic bags containing
1 Doz tortillas
2 Different daily newspapers
1 Crown Royal bag w/coffee mug

FOR ACT I:
1 Box with:
    1 1/2 Gal Milk
    1 Qt. Milk
    3 Packages string cheese

1 Box with:
    1 Box Saltines
    1 Box Corn Flakes
    1 Box Crisp Rice Cereal
    2 Cans Kidney Beans
    1 Box Hot Chocolate

FOR ACT II
4 Cardboard boxes with various papers, old newspapers, junk
1 Cardboard box with varied junk with a framed picture on top

AT ACT I INTERMISSION

Strike apples under counter

Strike Styrofoam cup

Strike ashtray

Strike Chavez's coffee cup (place OSR w/tortillas)

Strike Mooney's newspaper

Strike Silver's satchel (place OSR table)

Pour remaining coffee into empty decanter under counter, leaving only 1/2 cup in decanter – replace

Place black "X" Mug w/ coffee bag on counter

Empty coffee grounds from filter basket, replace with clean filter

Wipe out Silvers cup, place on cash register counter

Set Jamar's Rolling Stone Magazine on cash register counter

Wipe chicken scratches from chalk board

Place CD Boom Box on Deli Counter.

STRIKE FROM CENTER STAGE UNIT INTO LARGE BOX:

1 Box corn flakes

1 Box raisin bran

1 Box Rice Krispies

1 Bag flour

7 Cans chicken noodle soup

6 Cans tomato soup

6 Boxes macaroni & cheese

2 Jars of pickles

1 Jar mayonnaise

1 Jar mustard

1 Bottle ketchup

STRIKE INTO SMALLER BOX (To be set OSR for Jamar to enter with, top of Act II):

1 Box corn flakes
1 box raisin bran
1 Box Saltines
1 Box hot chocolate
Empty ALL money from cash register, place in money
   bag, place money bag in box

SCENE SHIFT BETWEEN ACT II & ACT III
(In our production, the play was produced in two acts. The
   following scene shift took place on stage:)

The character of Billy Moss enters through the front door
   with a small cardboard box. He strikes and sets the
   following:
Strikes narrow tray with Styrofoam cups and sugar cubes
   to below the counter
Set narrow tray with cup, cookies and towel to top of
   counter
Exchanges empty decanter with full decanter from below
   counter.
Strikes chess set into box
Places backgammon board, from below counter, to top of
   table
Strikes chimes from front door

At this time a crew member enters through the basement
   door:
Erases the Chalkboard completely
Strikes Boom Box to below the Deli Counter
Removes SMOKING PERMITTED sign
Replaces with SMOKING PROHIBITED sign
Strikes old phone to under counter

Sets cordless phone on counter

Billy Moss rotates the large CS unit to reveal fully stocked
shelves of name brand groceries

Crew Member rotates smaller unit to reveal shelves stocked
with video tapes and microwave popcorn

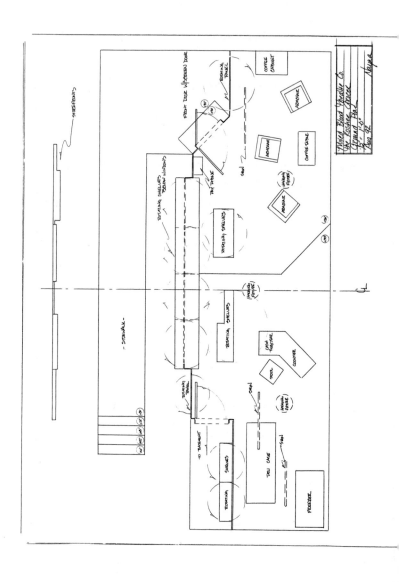